Praise for *The Decision Maker's Playbook*

'Each day, we make dozens, if not hundreds, of decisions. But every time we decide, we're bedevilled by biases that distort our thinking and direct us down blind alleys. In this timely work, Mueller and Dahr identify the roadblocks to efficient problem-finding and decision-making, and then prescribe solutions to overcome our worst instincts. This book is a must-have for all decision makers. And who isn't a decision maker?'

Daniel H. Pink, author of *When and Drive*

'Demands on leaders continue to increase. We all need tools to make the ideal choice in less-than-ideal conditions. Mueller and Dhar have the toolkit. Consider this your guide to doing big things well.'

Hon. Bill English, former Prime Minister of New Zealand

'Not happy with the quality of your decisions? Read this book. It's a treasure trove of tools for thinking more clearly.'

Rolf Dobelli, author of the million-copy bestseller
The Art of Thinking Clearly

'This engaging book contains an impressive, sweeping survey of the traps surrounding decision making and practical ways of avoiding them. The authors' playful approach makes it easy to engage in the exploration of a wide range of practical tools.'

Enrique Rueda-Sabater, former Head of Strategy,
The World Bank

The Decision Maker's Playbook

Pearson

At Pearson, we believe in learning – all kinds of learning for all kinds of people. Whether it's at home, in the classroom or in the workplace, learning is the key to improving our life chances.

That's why we're working with leading authors to bring you the latest thinking and best practices, so you can get better at the things that are important to you. You can learn on the page or on the move, and with content that's always crafted to help you understand quickly and apply what you've learned.

If you want to upgrade your personal skills or accelerate your career, become a more effective leader or more powerful communicator, discover new opportunities or simply find more inspiration, we can help you make progress in your work and life.

Every day our work helps learning flourish, and wherever learning flourishes, so do people.

To learn more, please visit us at **www.pearson.com/uk**

The Financial Times

With a worldwide network of highly respected journalists, *The Financial Times* provides global business news, insightful opinion and expert analysis of business, finance and politics. With over 500 journalists reporting from 50 countries worldwide, our in-depth coverage of international news is objectively reported and analysed from an independent, global perspective.

To find out more, visit **www.ft.com**

The Decision Maker's Playbook

12 mental tactics for thinking more clearly, navigating uncertainty and making smarter choices

Simon Mueller and Julia Dhar

Pearson

Harlow, England • London • New York • Boston • San Francisco • Toronto • Sydney • Dubai • Singapore • Hong Kong
Tokyo • Seoul • Taipei • New Delhi • Cape Town • São Paulo • Mexico City • Madrid • Amsterdam • Munich • Paris • Milan

PEARSON EDUCATION LIMITED
KAO Two
KAO Park
Harlow CM17 9SR
United Kingdom
Tel: +44 (0)1279 623623
Web: www.pearson.com/uk

First edition published 2019 (print and electronic)

© Pearson Education Limited 2019 (print and electronic)

ISBN: 978-1-292-12933-4 (print)
        978-1-292-12935-8 (PDF)
        978-1-292-12936-5 (ePub)

British Library Cataloguing-in-Publication Data
A catalogue record for the print edition is available from the British Library

Library of Congress Cataloging-in-Publication Data
A catalog record for the print edition is available from the Library of Congress

10 9 8 7 6 5 4 3 2 1
23 22 21 20 19

Cover design by Two Associates

Print edition typeset in 10/13 pt and SST by SPi Global

NOTE THAT ANY PAGE CROSS REFERENCES REFER TO THE PRINT EDITION

For my family and their unconditional love.
For Peter and his seminal mentorship.
For Anna and her relentless support.

Simon Mueller

For Granny and Jerry, and for Thatha.

Julia Dhar

CONTENTS

—

ABOUT THE AUTHORS

—

Simon Mueller is a Project Leader at Boston Consulting Group. Previously he served as the General Manager of the BCG Henderson Institute, the firm's strategy and macroeconomics think-tank. Simon has advised industrial and technology clients in North & Latin America, Europe and Asia, where he worked extensively on strategic and transformative projects focusing on advanced technologies such as robotics and 3D-printing. Simon is also co-founder of the global non-profit organization The Future Society, which develops governance solutions to ensure safety, fairness and shared prosperity in light of the rise of intelligent/autonomous systems.

Julia Dhar is a Partner at Boston Consulting Group. She co-founded and leads BeSmart, the firm's behavioral economics initiative, where she uses her expertise to make organizations more productive, profitable and happier. She has works extensively across the United States, the Middle East and Asia in the public and private sectors. Julia has also held policy and advisory roles in government, including Private Secretary to New Zealand's Minister of Finance.

ACKNOWLEDGEMENTS

—

This book would not have been published if it weren't for the help of many friends and supporters over the course of the five years it took from conception to publication. From framing the idea, selecting the 'mental tactics' that eventually found their way on to the pages, editorial suggestions and critiquing the narrative, we are very grateful for each and every contribution.

In particular, we would like to thank:

Richard Zeckhauser, whose infectious curiosity and intellectual brilliance served as the ignition spark for this project. Jieun Baek and Harry Begg, who helped us avoid some of the pitfalls as first-time authors. The prolific Cass Sunstein for his generous advice. Our editors Eloise Cook, David Crosby and Nicole Eggleton, with their excellent editorial suggestions and their imperturbable patience. Mary Trend for her critical eyes and red pen. Our friends and mentors John-Clark Levin, Craig White, Daichi Ueda, Alexander Goerlach, Johann Harnoss, Ofir Zigelman, Kevin Tan, Ben Hohne, Simon Hedlin-Larsson, Alex Bleier, Martin Guelck, Casper van der Ven, Denise Bailey-Castro, Stefan Woerner, Tom Lovering, Sek-loong Tan, Eric Gastfriend, Ben Scott, Arohi Jain, Christina Endruschat, Josh Cohen, Martin Reeves, Hannes Gurzki, Nico Miailhe, Lucas Ruengeler, Henry Alt-Haaker, Alan Iny, Maik Wehmeyer, Ambrose Gano, Stephan Wittig, Bjoern Lasse Herrmann, Benedikt Herles, Todd Shuster, Charlie Melvoin, Tobi Peyerl, Cyrus Hodes, Friederike von Reden, Nicolas Economou, Pepe Strathoff, Jannik Seger, Paul Chen, Torben Schulz, Eliot Glenn, Todd Elmer, Steffen von Buenau, Daniel Jahn, Elias Altman, David Hecker, Olivia Maurer, Michele Lunati, Iris Braun, Tony Peccatiello, Balthasar Mueller, Greg Manne, Ulrich Atz, Ed Walker, Valerie von der Tann, Beth Macy, Nafise Masoumi, Viola Mueller, Lolita Chuang, Christian Waeltermann, George Lehner and Nina Gussack, Nina Shapiro, Nidhi Sinha, Jonathan Willen, Alex Golden Cuevas, Jan-Peter Boeckstiegel, Patrick Daniel and Mette Moeller Joergensen.

INTRODUCTION
You're in a VUCA world now

—

Life is a sequence of decisions. Every day, we are faced with hundreds of choices: some small (what to eat for lunch), some substantial (where to live or where to work). The fear of 'the wrong choice' can be debilitating, while the amount of information required to make some choices can be overwhelming. We live in a world of ever-increasing complexity, and what we need is a better game plan – better maps of the territory of life, more robust mental models that effectively depict reality and help us make better decisions, faster. We call those maps 'mental tactics'.[1]

The book you are holding offers a selection of proven approaches to problem solving, decision making and implementation. It is for all of you who want to be more effective and efficient in your professional and personal lives. Mental tactics are cognitive shortcuts that help us identify patterns and relationships, avoid common cognitive errors, view the world from different angles, break down complex problems and take action.

The mental tactics portrayed in this book are distilled from various fields of research and practice, including statistics, politics, economics, systems theory, investing, operations research, game theory, medicine, psychology, military intelligence and philosophy. You will find that most mental tactics are applicable well beyond the disciplines in which they originated. Once you internalise them, you can apply them to a broad range of situations, from self-management to team effectiveness, to organisational leadership. They are as applicable to your personal dilemmas as your professional conundrums.

This book will help you to derive insights from data, overcome cognitive flaws, make more rational decisions and identify the fastest and most efficient path to implementation. In this book, we tend to address problems and decisions from an analytical standpoint. We favour simple, systematic approaches, which we illuminate for you through the checklists.

Our goal is to give you tools that are practical and immediately applicable. We wrote this book to share ideas and tools that we believe deserve a wider audience. Using the mental tactics has made a huge difference for the two of us, both in terms of the quality of our decisions and the speed and efficiency of our decision making. We started sharing these techniques with each other, our teams and wider network – and this book was born. We know the mental tactics here can help you in the same way and we are excited for this adventure you are about to come on with us. Let us begin!

Modern times

"You the people have the power, the power to create machines, the power to create happiness! You the people have the power to make this life free and beautiful, to make this life a wonderful adventure!" —

Charlie Chaplin[2]

One of the most iconic scenes in the history of film depicts the Little Tramp, played by Charlie Chaplin, fixing products on an assembly line (see above). Over time, Little Tramp himself becomes more and more machine-like, determined to accomplish one thing and one thing only: wrenching screws on gadgets that pass by on a conveyor belt, over and over again.

In an attempt to increase efficiency, the factory supervisor turns a lever to speed up the assembly line. Little Tramp hastens to keep up and grows increasingly more desperate as he races to complete the task against the ever faster tide of work.

Today, we find more and more monotonous labour tasks completed by algorithms or robots. While the industrial environments in Chaplin's film focused on controlling every movement of the worker (one scene shows Little Tramp as a guinea pig for a machine that feeds workers so they never have to stop working), today's workplace environment is often quite the opposite. Instead of one single repetitive task, most of us face a new kind of frustration: the overwhelming abundance of information, options and stimulation.

The increasing complexity of work and the break-neck speed at which business is conducted have permeated all aspects of life. Disruptive events happen more and more frequently, while social and digital transformations open up new opportunities for collaboration and action on an unprecedented scale. We're living in what the US Army War College calls a VUCA world – Volatile, Uncertain, Complex and Ambiguous.[3]

Volatile	Uncertain
Unstable and unpredictable change	Implications of an event are unclear
Complex	Ambiguous
Elaborate networks of info; not immediately understandable	Cause and effect unclear; future predicitons difficult

In this world, we need new tools to help us make the right choices. We need strategies to solve questions such as the following:

- What career path should I pursue that withstands technological automation and obsolescence?
- How do I make wise financial choices, from buying a house to investing in education?
- How can my company thrive in an environment of ongoing disruption?
- How do I determine the most efficient use of my team's time and resources?

In these times of high uncertainty and complexity, our natural tendency is to overestimate risks and discount rewards. As a consequence, we dramatically shorten our time horizons and shift our attention to what we can get *today*, since the longer term seems so fraught with uncertainty, even though the potential rewards may be much greater. Given these tendencies, how do we make informed decisions? How do we prioritise? Little Tramp needed one tool, a wrench, to try to stay on top of his work. Today, we need an entire toolkit to perform successfully.

There is a biological reason for this. Our built-in decision making capacity isn't adapted to many of the environments we find ourselves in today. The human brain evolved via evolutionary mechanisms over millions of years to perceive and prioritise certain pieces of information, identify relationships and make decisions. Our education and experience teach us methods to enhance these built-in processes in some cases, and overcome them in others. Yet our own common sense, and an ever-growing body of social psychology and decision-science research, shows that we still often go awry. Why? While our evolutionary programming and past experience go a long way towards helping us make good decisions, our professional and personal environments are changing too fast for our education (our software), let alone our brains (our hardware) to keep pace.

Demands on leaders are increasing

This change in context brings with it enhanced requirements for managers and leaders. Competition for jobs has increased due to the globalisation of the workforce. Having a top-notch degree from a prestigious university is no longer sufficient to cement one's place in society. Rather, it is the ability to be flexible and adapt to changing requirements, keeping a cool head in fast-paced times, and deciding rationally yet emphatically.

Building and maintaining an edge in thinking and decision making is far from easy. It takes commitment, effort and practice. Rigid models and fixed blueprints will soon cease to work because the environment is changing very quickly. Our mental models need to adapt to new contexts and be flexible enough to be tuned and adjusted for individual situations.

In an age of real-time news and information, leaders are not only required to make the *right* decisions, they also need to make them *fast*. They will benefit from building a muscle memory of mental frameworks and methods that allow them drastically to shorten the time required to analyse, decide and act on information.

How to read this book

The Decision Maker's Playbook is not your typical non-fiction book. We will avoid long prose and stories and instead give you a highly visual and intuitive introduction to tactics that we value and use ourselves. To make it easier to read, each chapter (with the exception of Chapters Zero and Thirteen) will follow a similar structure:

- **Benefits** outline the specific advantages of each mental tactic.
- **Checklists** provide step-by-step instructions.
- **Further examples** demonstrate how the mental tactic is used in different circumstances.
- **The bottom line** summarises the chapter and distils its key insights.

Each chapter is self-contained. That means you can flip through the book and read the chapters you find most intriguing. There is, however, a logical arc to the structure of this book, resembling the way we naturally navigate the world and solve problems – observing, analysing, crafting a solution and executing it:

- Part 1 is about learning how to collect evidence and direct your attention to the most important facts and observations. You will learn to focus on previously overlooked but essential pieces of data and information.

- Part 2 presents mental tactics that connect the dots and establish causal links between facts or events. This includes separating the signal from the noise, and discerning the nature of causal relationships which go beyond mere correlations.

- Part 3 focuses on the tools required to craft a solution to design an approach that will overcome a challenge. This step involves mental tactics that help you think about opening up options, and includes practical decision-making frameworks.

- Part 4 covers mental tactics that will enable you to implement the solution in an effective way, and provide you with techniques to make it happen.

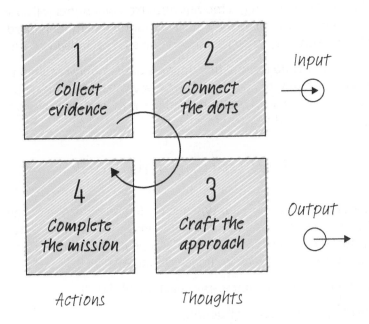

Some important caveats

What are mental tactics? View them as thinking and acting tools. They have a broad range of applicability in your personal life and at work. They are neither one size fits all nor plug and play. The following points are particularly important to keep in mind to maximise the benefit you will get from this book:

- **Mental tactics are meant to complement, not to substitute:** they enhance the way you already interact with reality, how you make sense of the world, and your personal style of decision making. Mental tactics introduce and share a new perspective and a new set of tools for solving problems, but they aren't able to completely overhaul your problem-solving approach.

- **The list of mental tactics in this book is far from exhaustive:** we necessarily had to make a selection when considering which tools to include in this book and which to leave out. That was far from easy, and many useful approaches didn't make the cut. This book is meant to provide novel and effective approaches, not be the standard reference for any kind of problem. As we were thinking about what to include, we applied the following lenses:

  - *Proven practicality*: you could call both of us professional problem-solvers. We work with companies and governments to find solutions to difficult problems. All of the mental tactics here have helped us solve problems in our daily work. But few of them *originated* in the corporate world, or are even unique to our line of work. Instead, they are taken from a wide array of domains. Even though other tactics were intellectually intriguing and academically promising, we have refrained from including them here (even though sometimes we really wanted to, for example Bayesian inference). It is meant to be a book *by* practitioners *for* practitioners. We want you to *apply* the mental tactics, not just *think* about them.

  - *Generally underrated*: we prefer to explore lesser-known mental tactics that we have observed in highly effective thinkers and decision makers (such as thinking on the margin). In addition, we aim to shine a light on those tactics that are intuitively known but rarely used effectively, such as a deep understanding of how to shape incentive systems. Some of the ideas might be familiar to you, but you will find them cast in a new light in this book.

Our goal is to equip you with the right instruments to help you make sound decisions, take action effectively and lead with confidence.

Chapter Zero

What's your problem?

A problem well put is half solved.
John Dewey

FRAME YOUR PROBLEM FIRST

Before we can start pondering potential solutions, we need to familiarise ourselves with what a problem actually is. Let's use the working definition: a problem is a question in search of an answer or a solution. Here is what's typically not recognised: asking good questions is paramount for good problem-solving. In other words, problem-framing is part of problem-solving.

That is why this book purposely has a Chapter Zero. Often, when confronted with a new dilemma or opportunity, our instinct is to dive in – to start gathering data, forming hypotheses, marshalling resources or testing solutions. All of these activities are critically important – and we will come to them. Before we do, though, let's add a new step to your decision-making playbook. Step zero: frame the problem appropriately.

1. Problems don't just exist – we actively choose them

It is widely assumed that problems simply exist. They don't need to be found, they simply impose themselves on us. This is a mistaken belief. Picking a problem to solve is almost always an active process. This is true for any problem, regardless of whether it emerges in your private or professional life.

Let's start with an example that we see all the time. At any given moment in time, a large corporation faces a range of different challenges: ongoing intellectual property lawsuits, the uncertain development of customer demand and preferences, new market entrants and pivoting competitors, talent shortages and challenges with leadership transition, potential strikes, political uncertainties. The list goes on and on.

The sheer amount of potential issues makes it impossible for management to focus on all of them at any given moment. A choice has to be made. Often, this choice is driven by circumstances or intuition. A former CFO is appointed to take over as CEO and, because she tends to see things through her finance lens, she quickly identifies the most pressing issue to be creeping costs. A cost-cutting project is the natural answer. Or say the department head has just got back from leadership training, convinced that leadership skills are the constraining bottleneck in his department. He promptly requires everyone in his team to sign up for personalised leadership coaching.

It is easy to see that this department head has actively picked a problem, namely lack of leadership skills. Problem-framing is always a choice. Your boss might choose the problem for you, but you have more control than you think over how to respond.

Consider the public arena as a different example. The discursive process we call democracy can also be seen as an exercise in problem-framing. Candidates run on different platforms that emphasise certain problems and tone down others. They suggest solutions for the problems they have actively identified, then the media provides a platform for public discourse about it. In this arena, newspapers, public intellectuals and commentators compete for attention. The electorate forms their view and elects the political candidate whose programme is best aligned with their beliefs.

Next time, before you jump into problem-solving mode right away, take a step back to reflect on *who* decided that the issue you are facing is a problem worth solving, and think about *why* they did so, and what their perspective might be.

2. Not every problem should be solved

Problems seem apparent when you first encounter them. Remember our new CEO from above? Early in her tenure, she discovered that some of her sales people seem to be very extravagant on their expenses. A few have repeatedly booked pricey flights, while others seem to be requesting reimbursement for fancy dinners with potential clients.

Clearly, tightening the expense policy in order to cut costs seems reasonable.

But if you think about potential second and third-order effects, this might not necessarily be the smartest idea. A tighter expense policy will curtail expensive flights and limit the expenses for dinners with clients, but may also increase the effort and time spent by your whole team itemising receipts and justifying expenditures. Not only does this take the team's effort away from other more productive activities, but it may also dissuade them from setting up some sales dinners or trips in the first place.

On the margin, the net effect may be lowering your sales team's commercial success. So statistically, the foregone profits could easily dwarf the additional expenses. And to be clear, we are not claiming that 'over-expensing' is not a problem. It is. But in the above case this problem might be better left unresolved because the only (or typical) solution open to you creates worse problems.

It seems self-evident that problems are – in absolute terms – *bad* and need resolution. But just like the problem of expense reimbursements going overboard, that doesn't necessarily need to be the case. Yes, the *first-order* consequence is bad: excessive expenses directly lower your bottom line profits. But minimising the threshold for your sales team to visit high-value clients, even when it comes with expensive travel, might be net-positive if you think about *second-order* consequences.

3. Not every problem needs to be solved immediately

Many problems seem to require *immediate* solutions. But often we confuse importance with urgency. In fact, a consumer research team led by Zhu, Yang and Hsee, found a significant 'urgency effect' – a mindset of focusing on urgent rather than important tasks. Their experiments showed that test subjects tend to prioritise tasks with a lower expected reward over tasks with a higher reward, when the former were merely classified as urgent.[4]

A prioritisation model, such as the well-known Eisenhower matrix, will help you decide which problems to tackle in what order. It may not surprise you to learn that Dwight D. Eisenhower, a five-star general, supreme commander of the Allied Expeditionary Forces during the Second World War and US President, was a master organiser and productivity guru in his time. He saw past the blinders of urgency, coining the phrase, "What is important is seldom urgent, and what is urgent is seldom important."[5]

To apply this matrix, ask yourself:

1 How important is this problem? Left unaddressed, how bad would the impact actually be?

2 How urgent is the problem? In other words, how time-sensitive is it that the problem be solved? Will addressing it soon prevent a further spread of its consequences? Or is it simply a low-importance problem that is trying hard to compete for your attention?

Using a simple 2x2 matrix can help you get a clear view over your priorities.

Urgency

	Low	High
Low	Don't do	Delegate
High	Schedule/ do later	Focus right now

Importance

Only those problems in the high/high category need immediate attention. Those that are important but not urgent should be scheduled or 'time-boxed', whereas those that are urgent but not important should be delegated, if possible.

4. Not every problem needs to be solved by you

A surprisingly large number of problems, if left to their own devices, appear to take care of themselves. Have you ever found an abandoned, one-month-old to-do list with a few items checked off and the rest still unchecked? In all likelihood, most of the unchecked tasks have already been taken care of. Either you or someone else completed them, or they have simply become obsolete.

What's the lesson here?

Next time, before noting down your intentions on your to-do list, ask yourself what would happen if you didn't tackle this problem. The what-would-happen-otherwise is known as the 'counterfactual'.

Take a career choice example. When asked about their life goals, many of today's students rank 'making the world a better place' high on their lists. There are at least two ways for them to accomplish this: either by directly improving the lives of other people or the environment (as a doctor, political campaigner or aid worker), or indirectly by enabling others to do better or more work (for example, by giving to charity).

The impact one can have by working directly on important causes can often be lower than the impact one can have by accepting a high-paying job and giving a substantial amount to effective charities.[6] Because many of the directly impactful 'doing good' positions are in high demand, there's a lot of competition for them. If one doesn't take that job as an aid worker, someone else who is most likely similarly skilled will. So the real impact from that career choice is most likely smaller than its perceived impact.

Say you are a medical doctor working in accident and emergency. Over the course of your career, you save a thousand lives. But if you hadn't taken that job, chances are that someone else would have taken it instead of you. The real impact of your choice to become a medical doctor and working to save lives is probably lower than you think.[7] As a simple example, say you would save a thousand lives over the course of your career as a doctor. You are well-trained, efficient, and have a strong sense of the good you can do in the world. But Mary, Joe and Tom happen to live in the same city and finish medical school in the same year. Coming from similar backgrounds and having attended the same university, they would be able to save 980, 950 and 720 lives respectively. If there's sufficient competition for the position in the Accident and Emergency Department (and the hospital is able to choose the most effective doctor), your *marginal* impact is 'only' 20 lives. Why? In your absence, Mary would have chosen the role, saving 980 lives.

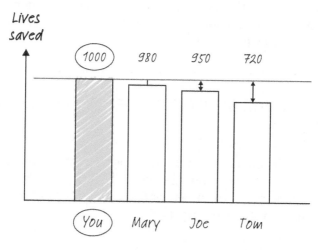

On the other hand, there's typically less competition for the next donation. Charities are more cash-strapped than talent-strapped, so making a monetary donation is often more effective.

CHECKLIST

How to approach problems

 REMEMBER THAT FRAMING A PROBLEM IS ALWAYS AN ACTIVE TASK

Problems don't just pop up, they are actively chosen and framed. It's your choice to accept a problem, and another choice to actively develop a solution.

 ASK WHO HAS AN INTEREST IN SOLVING IT AND WHO HAS NO INTEREST IN IT BEING SOLVED

Problems are inherently political. Some people benefit from a certain problem being solved, while others suffer from it. Take climate change. It is catastrophic for many of us, and potentially for humanity as a whole, yet opposing climate change policies could be beneficial for select countries or organisations that are benefiting from the status quo. Asking *cui bono* (who benefits?) helps you understand the interest dynamics behind the selection and framing of the problems that present themselves to you.

 THINK ABOUT THE SECOND-ORDER EFFECTS OF SOLVING A PROBLEM

Problems never exist in isolation. Just as in the example with the expense policy above, there are second-order effects to every solution. Ask yourself if a problem is actually just a side effect of some bigger phenomena which may not require a solution. Would solving the problem just create more problems than leaving it be?

PRIORITISE YOUR PROBLEMS WITH THE EISENHOWER MATRIX

Not every problem needs to be dealt with *immediately.* The Eisenhower matrix helps you revisit your priorities by looking at importance and urgency more deliberately. Use it to select those problems that need immediate attention and de-prioritise those of lower priority.

 ## ASK WHAT WOULD HAPPEN IN THE ABSENCE OF YOU SOLVING IT

Thinking about the counterfactual (what would happen if I didn't do it?) is an important step to evaluate what your incremental impact really is. If a problem gets taken care of anyway, you might think about focusing your efforts on different problems.

HOW TO FIND GOOD PROBLEM STATEMENTS

Let's say you own a small business that sells wooden toys for children. You love your work and the positive feedback you receive from parents all over the country. But as this business is your only source of income, you need to make prudent decisions.

Your initial problem statement is "How can I sell more?" Of course, there are a number of ways this can be accomplished. You might think of ramping up advertising, launching a content marketing campaign, a word-of-mouth initiative, or lowering the price points of your products. All of these have the potential to increase your sales.

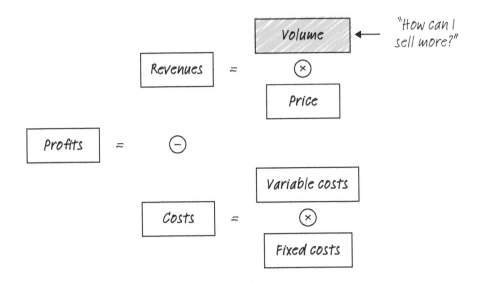

But what you are *really* after is not sales, but profits. Restating the problem as "How do I increase long-term profits?" will open up completely new options. Can you, for example, *increase* the price and use the proceeds for additional advertising? Can you develop new low-cost or simplified versions of your blockbuster products to increase volume? Can you save costs by renegotiating the volume and prices of the raw materials you buy?

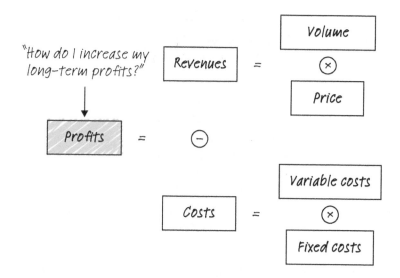

By changing the problem focus from sales to profits, you have reframed the problem. You broadened your scope by focusing on the financial metric that is downstream from sales. And because the way we frame problems typically defines the way we analyse them, reframing allows us to see new solutions. If our initial problem framing is one-sided or narrow, we might only be able to find a suboptimal solution. Instead of the global optimum (the best solution for the true problem), we will be stuck at a local optimum (the best answer *given the limited scope of the problem statement*).

Symptoms versus root causes

Are you observing the *symptom* of a larger phenomenon? A broken leg hurts, but pain is just a symptom. Morphine injections can certainly suppress the pain, but they do nothing to tackle the root cause. Ignoring that might lead to tragic outcomes.

Say you are the office manager of a software company. Over the last few months, you have noticed a large amount of trash in the office – empty cups, tin cans, napkins and paper all over the place. Naturally, you assume the fault to lie with the office workers. Your initial problem statement is "How can we educate our staff to be cleaner?"

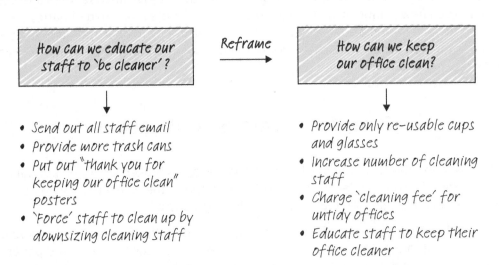

How can we educate our
staff to 'be cleaner'?

- Send out all staff email
- Provide more trash cans
- Put out "thank you for
  keeping our office clean"
  posters
- 'Force' staff to clean up by
  downsizing cleaning staff

This problem frame will result in a number of good ideas. But have you really dug down to the root cause? The cause of the mess is not just to do with the people. It's also the stuff that can be carelessly left on tables and the floor, such as single-use coffee cups, plastic wrapping or paper. Change your problem frame to "How can we keep our office clean?" in order to widen the aperture for solutions.

How can we educate our   Reframe   How can we keep
staff to 'be cleaner'?   ———————▶   our office clean?

- Send out all staff email   - Provide only re-usable cups
- Provide more trash cans   and glasses
- Put out "thank you for   - Increase number of cleaning
  keeping our office clean"   staff
  posters   - Charge 'cleaning fee' for
- 'Force' staff to clean up by   untidy offices
  downsizing cleaning staff   - Educate staff to keep their
                                          office cleaner

By doing this, a wider range of potential solutions open up to you – and what used to be the original framing will just become one aspect among many others. We will dive into root causes and how to analyse them in more detail later.

CHECKLIST

How to find new problem frames

 BRING MORE, DIVERSE BRAINS TO THE TABLE

Bring in people who weren't exposed to the problem before. They are not caught in the weeds and can bring fresh thinking to it. Ideally, find people who know *enough about the problem* but don't have a *vested interest* in the solution. In our experience, it is these people who are most objective and helpful in reframing the problem.

 HARVEST THE POWER OF INDIVIDUALS WITHOUT GETTING CAUGHT UP IN GROUP THINK

Many brainstorming sessions fail because one person dominates the session. This can be avoided by asking participants to *write down* their reframing ideas first, and only then *discussing* the ideas with the full team. When reframing problems, wording really matters. Make sure you allow enough time for your team to think about individual solutions before you review them in the larger group. Allow at least five minutes.

Start with a short brainstorming session and ask everyone to write down as many problem frames as possible. It is important that they are full sentences. Initially, don't evaluate, simply ask your team to churn out as many ideas as possible while withholding judgement.

 ASK PROBING QUESTIONS TO STIMULATE THINKING

Questions can help shape the definition of your problem. Make sure you only start asking questions or giving prompts *after* the initial silent brainstorming session is over. Examples for questions are:

- What is the *true root cause* of the problem? What are just *symptoms*?
- What would happen if you *narrowed* the scope? What if you *broadened* it?
- *Who benefits* from this problem being solved? Who suffers from it? Who is indifferent?

############### THE BOTTOM LINE ###############

Problems don't just exist, we actively choose and frame them. Good decision makers ask the question zero first: What's my problem? Reflect on the framing of the problem: *Who* framed it? What are their underlying interests? And then think hard about whether the problem would benefit from reframing. Should it be solved at all? Immediately? By me?

Part 1

Collect evidence

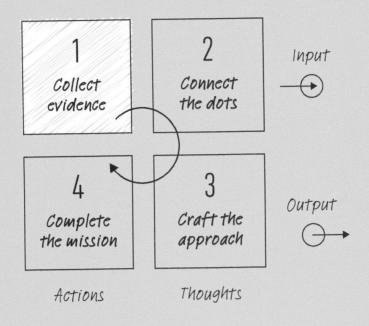

1 Collect evidence	2 Connect the dots	Input →⊕→
4 Complete the mission	3 Craft the approach	Output ⊕→
Actions	Thoughts	

We are overwhelmed by information. Not only is the amount growing, but the *pace* of growth is ever-increasing. Buckminster Fuller, a systems theorist, noticed that until 1900 the sum of human knowledge doubled approximately every century. By the early 1950s, knowledge was doubling every 25 years. Now, with the rise of connected devices, that number will be further compressed with the data stream produced by the rise of connected 'Internet of Things' devices coming online.

At the same time, knowledge, which we build by absorbing and using information, remains essential for making decisions and taking action in all our endeavours. An increase in information is not the same as an increase in knowledge. And an increase in knowledge is not the same as an increase in actionable intelligence.

The amount of news is steadily increasing, but so is the amount of false, misleading or inaccurate information. Particularly in the age of social media, this is particularly dangerous, as misleading and false information spreads and disseminates oftentimes faster than any correction released afterwards.

In the 2016 US presidential election cycle, one incident in particular stood out. In the autumn of 2016, a number of right-leaning internet users fabricated rumours that the Democratic Party was linked to a paedophilia ring. In a country divided along partisan lines, the message fell on fruitful ground, and spread through forums such as 4chan and Reddit to a broader audience on social media. A pizza restaurant based in Washington DC, that was allegedly involved in this conspiracy, started receiving hundreds of threats from the theory's believers. In the end, it culminated in an incident in which an armed man entered the pizza parlour and shot three rounds from his AR-15-style rifle. Mercifully, no one was injured.

Fakes disguised as facts are an immense problem for society. At best, they are confusing and distracting and, at worst, they are deliberately misleading and manipulative. In this first part of the book, we will discuss how we collect data and observations that inform our opinions and decisions. We will focus on the cognitive distortions that cloud our view, make us ignore important facts and skew our beliefs about the world. Using specific examples, we will analyse the distortions and what is required to overcome them in a systematic way.

Unfortunately, our cognitive facilities are often limited by biases that make it difficult to gather the right information and use it effectively. Typically, we only notice information that confirms our existing preconceptions, and we surround ourselves with people who share our beliefs. This leads to a warped perspective that psychologists call 'confirmation bias'.[8] What we think about also informs a lot of what we see. People who think a lot about what clothes to wear also pay attention to other people's clothing choices. People who have recently read a news story about a plane crash overestimate the risk of plane crashes. We find it easiest to recall facts, objects or concepts that we have recently been reminded of. This bias is known as the 'availability heuristic'. Nobel Laureate Daniel Kahneman, who along with Amos Tversky, broke new ground in behavioural economics, calls this' WYSIATI – What You See Is All There Is.'[9]

Blind spots are tricky. Not only are we *missing information,* but we're also *not aware that we're missing it.* Our brain typically fills in the gaps by piecing together information to create a line of thought that skips over the blind spots. As a result, we believe that we've taken everything important into account in making a particular decision, even if we're missing critical pieces of the puzzle.

These cognitive flaws make us oblivious to the information we need to make smart decisions and prevent us from effectively using the information we do have. Still, there are some steps we can take to counter our cognitive limitations. In this part of the book, we will introduce strategies for uncovering your blind spots and correcting false beliefs.

Chapter One

—

Illuminate your blind spots

Admit what you don't know and correct your wrong beliefs

We're generally overconfident in our opinions and our impressions and judgments.

Daniel Kahneman, *Thinking, Fast and Slow*

BENEFITS OF THIS MENTAL TACTIC

Collecting and processing data is the first step in solving problems. However, the path towards building a robust and accurate 'fact base' as a basis for solid decision making is littered with pitfalls. This mental tactic helps you unmask your blind spots and calibrate the confidence you have in your beliefs.

Because of its fundamental nature, this mental tactic can be used whenever you are trying to understand and solve an analytical problem.

ADMIT WHAT YOU DON'T KNOW

When Jamie started driving cabs for a licensed taxi company in 2005, it seemed like a no-brainer. New York: the booming city of affluent professionals who need a ride everywhere, at all times of the day. In the beginning, he found himself easily making more than $200 per day. A few years later, he decided to double down on this lucrative opportunity. With his goal of financial independence in sight, he borrowed more than $250,000 to buy his own taxi medallion (licence system in the USA).

Ten years later, Jamie found himself unable to pay off his debt. As more and more passengers switched to apps such as Uber or Lyft, Jamie's daily salary dropped considerably. Even though he avoided the peak of medallion prices (in 2014 the market rate was well above a million dollars), he still shared the same fate as thousands of other taxi drivers who just didn't see the age of app services coming.[10] In June 2018, the *New York Post* reported that prices had fallen to $160,000–$250,000 each.[11]

The 'sharing economy' has flipped the world of mobility on its head. Getting into a car with an unknown person? Sleeping in a stranger's bed? Just a few years ago, this was unthinkable. Today, these models are mainstream and continue to hurt established players and businesses.

Is there a way of systematically uncovering one's blind spots and identifying wrong beliefs? That is exactly what this is about:

- First, how to detect true blind spots – areas devoid of information that are important for decision making.

- Second, how to spot and overcome incorrect beliefs.

Beliefs about the state and mechanics of the world

Hands-down the most important ingredient for problem solving and decision making is holding beliefs that are in accordance with fact and reality.

Our beliefs (or in the absence of beliefs, blind spots) fall into three categories (or classes):

1 **Beliefs about the current states of the world (today):** if you arrive at the airport at 7am, believing your flight departs at 8.20am when, in fact, it took off at 6.20am, you are holding wrong beliefs about the current state of the world (and were punished for it immediately by missing your plane).

2 **Beliefs about the causal mechanics of the world:** the incorrect belief that vaccinations could cause autism prevented many parents from immunising their children. Locally, this can lead to the immunisation rate falling below the threshold required to prevent communicable diseases from spreading. In some places, such as Minnesota, anti-vaccine activists managed to convince a critical number of parents not to vaccinate their children, which caused over 70 confirmed cases of measles in 2017.[12]

3 **Beliefs about future states of the world (predictions):** if you place a bet on a race horse winning, you believe in the relative strength of your favourite relative to its competition (Class 1) *and* in organised horse-racing as a reliable mechanism to accurately determine the racing times of horses (Class 2).

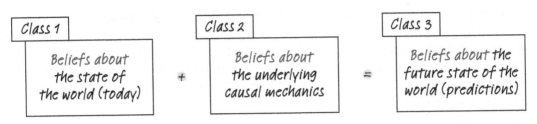

Class 1
Beliefs about the state of the world (today)

+

Class 2
Beliefs about the underlying causal mechanics

=

Class 3
Beliefs about the future state of the world (predictions)

As shown, the third class of belief is typically a function of the first two classes of beliefs (either implicitly or explicitly).

Let's revisit Jamie the taxi driver's situation. Which beliefs could have influenced his decision? He might have:

- underestimated customers' preferences for taxi-sharing services (Class 1) or the pace at which customers' preferences changed (Class 2)

- overestimated the ability of the taxi lobby to influence regulation towards maintaining the status quo (Class 1)

- overestimated the growth in city population, per-capita spending and the subsequent increase in demand of passenger miles (mix of Class 1 and Class 2).

Of course, at this point we can only speculate, but any or all of these beliefs could have prompted Jamie to predict a rosy future for the taxi industry and therefore invest in a taxi medallion.

Predictably wrong

Whenever we form beliefs about the state and mechanics of the world, uncertainty is involved in some form or another. This should not come as a surprise. We simply cannot know or process everything.

However, some of our cognitive limitations are structural (and hence predictable). They fool us again and again in similar ways, and distort our thinking. These limitations are known as cognitive biases and have attracted a growing community of scientists working in fields such as behavioural economics and neuroscience.

For example, it can be shown experimentally that we tend to:

- be influenced by the first bit of information we acquire about a certain topic and are unlikely to move away from it – the 'anchoring effect'

- update our beliefs insufficiently when presented with new evidence – the 'belief revision effect'

- completely neglect probability when making a decision under uncertainty.

We will take a more comprehensive look at some of the most important cognitive biases in the next chapter.[13]

Admitting to being wrong isn't fashionable

Not only are we biased in multiple ways, we are also subject to strong social norms that are difficult to overcome and change our views. Admitting to not knowing an answer or to being wrong is socially stigmatised. If a CIO quotes incorrect figures during quarterly performance reports, you can be sure they will be called to account. So-called strong leaders are often perceived as strong simply because they refuse to voice natural human uncertainty. They are required to know the way and take bold leaps forward.[14]

It is typically not humility that is criticised, but an assumed mental attitude or capability. For example, saying "I don't know" might either be taken as "I'm not *able* to know" which could indicate cognitive limitations, or as "I don't *want* to know," which suggests a lack of motivation to find out.

////// DIFFERENT TYPES OF IGNORANCE //////

It helps to classify the different types of ignorance in order to spot them quickly. The following matrix separates truthfulness of belief and perceived level of confidence.

- **Truthfulness of belief:** is something you believe *objectively* true? Or is it false?

- **Level of confidence:** are you *highly confident* that you are holding a truthful belief, or is your confidence level *low*? For instance, do you know *for sure* that your co-worker will be promoted because his superior just confided it to you? Or is your belief just a wild guess based on speculations about your colleague's performance?

Level of confidence

	High	Low
True	"See? I was 100% sure all along"	"Turns out I was right –how lucky"
False	"Oops, I was so sure"	"Well, it was just a wild guess anyway"

Belief is ...

As you navigate the world around you and make hundreds of decisions every day, you will find yourself most frequently in the top-left quadrant. To take a profane example: you can be pretty sure that the coffee-maker will not explode when you turn it on in the morning.

But be aware of the bottom-left quadrant, the hallmark of overconfidence. As the prices of residential homes continued to increase throughout the 1990s and the early 2000s, few people were aware of the risk of a slowdown (let alone crash). Yet that's exactly what happened, and it triggered a domino-effect of defaults and foreclosures, which took a heavy hit on banks and then the economy as a whole. Exposure to only one trend direction, namely upwards, made many investors complacent and overconfident.

Overconfidence is also at play when it comes to evaluating our own skills, which is known as the 'Dunning-Kruger effect'.[15] Those who are lower skilled often rate their skill level as very high, which means that they are essentially lacking the capability to correctly judge their performance. While there is some correlation between a person's estimation of their own skills and their actual competency, it is smaller than one might suppose: the top 25% of test-takers are underconfident in how well they did at a given test, while the bottom 25% of test-takers are overconfident.

What if we haven't formed a belief yet, possibly because we aren't aware of the existence of something? For example, you might not have gathered knowledge about the risks of Artificial Intelligence, simply due to a lack of awareness. The matrix below can be informative.

Awareness

	Aware	Not aware
Known	Known knowns	Unknown Knowns (not applicable)
Unknown	Known unknowns	Unknown unknowns

Knowledge of facts

Let's start with the top-left quadrant, the 'known knowns'.[16] These are typically relatively straightforward situations that are both deterministic and display clear causal relationships. Problems and solutions in this field are typically undisputed. For example, take the example of a flat tyre on your car. Not only is it clear what the problem is (you will notice its deflation), but often the cause is visible as well (a nail or a rip). In addition, the problem *solution* is mostly undisputed: change your tyre.

Let's move on to the bottom-left quadrant, the 'known unknowns'. Typical examples for problems in this category are textbook questions. Hence, when you encounter them, expertise is the best remedy. Before reading the maths textbook chapter on integration you don't know how to integrate the formula, but after you work through it, it's easy to figure out the answer. On the surface, problems in this category can seem daunting and complicated, with multiple possible 'right' answers. But if you look past the fine details, you'll see that the type of problem has been solved before.

The third category in the bottom right are the real blind spots. These 'unknown unknowns' are arguably the trickiest ones. By its very definition, we don't know what we don't know. Hence, there can't be any specific advice on what to do with the items in this category, because they are simply unknown. However, there are creative ways of surfacing them. Using some of the approaches featured below will help you imagine the unimagined, and move unknown unknowns from the bottom-right to the bottom-left.

DETECTING BLIND SPOTS AND AVOIDING FALSE BELIEFS

1. Understand how your mind works

There are three mental enemies that make overcoming blind spots and changing incorrect beliefs particularly challenging. We have already touched on some of them above. Our mind has the tendency to:

- automatically look out for evidence *confirming* our preconceptions
- fill white spots with *well-sounding* (i.e. plausible and believable) stories
- be better at finding fault with what's in front of our eyes than finding out what's *missing.*

Let's talk about the first one. It is called 'selective cognition'. We tend to gather evidence that confirms our existing values and beliefs rather than evidence that challenges it. To overcome this, you need to be aware of what values you believe to be true and what beliefs about the world you hold. This is true for both your own perception and the media sources you chose to consume, but also the (social) media sources themselves.

Second, our mind masks white spots with well-sounding stories. And it does so not only before we make a decision, but also after it. In one fascinating experiment, scientists set up a tasting booth for tea and jam, and passers-by were asked which combination they preferred after tasting. But after they made their decision, the participants were asked to sample again and verbally explain what led them to the choice they made. Unbeknown to them, by that time, the researchers had switched the contents of the jars, which now contained the exact *opposite* of what the test subjects chose. No more than a third of all participants noticed the switch.[17] Our mind quickly fills in the gaps, even if it doesn't quite match with our experience.

Finally, it is much easier to find fault with what is readily in front of our eyes, what is *known*, than it is to identify what is *missing.* This happens to your authors all the time, for example, when reviewing documents or presentations. Figuring out what is *missing* (what argument or assumption *should* be there but isn't) is an order of magnitude more difficult than *correcting* what is incorrect (for example, a false statement or illogical assumption).

2. Try to make the best possible argument for the other side

It is easy to fall in love with our own perspectives and world views. We create positions that suit us and then defend them. We get attached to them.

However, it is generally good practice to *make the best possible argument for the other side.* Give them the benefit of the doubt: let them (or yourself) make the best and most convincing argument for *why you are wrong.* The more you are engaged in trying to build *their case,* the more you are not only finding holes in your system of beliefs, but also enhancing your empathy for the other side. Daniel Dennett, a well-known thinker who explores the philosophy of mind and consciousness, wrote: "You should attempt to re-express your target's position so clearly, vividly, and fairly, that your target says, 'Thanks, I wish I'd thought of putting it that way.'"[18]

3. Be humble

Nurturing humility is one of the most effective ways of keeping overconfidence in check. Richard Feynman, the great physicist and educator, once said: "I'm smart enough to know I'm dumb."[19] Humility is about adjusting one's attitude towards admitting that one could be wrong, actively asking for advice, and finding ways to double-check beliefs and judgements.

4. Attach probabilities to your beliefs and regularly calibrate them

Instead of just comparing the instances in which you were right with the ones in which you thought you were, you can be more specific. One way to practise everyday humility when dealing with beliefs is to attach probabilities to them.

In the Appendix, we provide you with a proven confidence calibration method and showcase an example.

5. Place bets on your beliefs

There's a saying that talk is cheap – and in our social media-driven world, we're talking more than ever. It's easy to make unsupported claims or wild guesses about the world we live in when nothing is at stake. But what if we hold ourselves to higher standards, putting consequences in place to encourage us to think critically and probingly about our opinions?

One easy way to do this is to get into the habit of placing bets on our beliefs and predictions. If an expensive dinner or a hundred bucks depends on our accuracy, we might think more carefully about our answers. Alex Taborrok, a professor at George Mason University, put it neatly when he called bets "a tax on bullshit".[20]

6. Adopt a sceptic's mindset

Collins Dictionary's entry of the year 2017 was 'fake news'. Used as a weapon to attack unfavourable reports and the media at large, it spread quickly.

It's clear that we as problem solvers need to be on our guard against fake news. But first, we need to learn how to recognise it.

Claims should be analysed on two levels:

1 Is the claim *in itself* plausible?

2 Is the *source* trustworthy and not conflicted?

Let's start with the first point. We tend to use our intuitive knowledge of the world to assess how plausible a claim is. The better a claim fits with what we already believe of the world, the more plausible it is. The less it does, the more evidence it requires. In the words of Carl Sagan: "Extraordinary claims deserve extraordinary evidence."[21]

Now on to the second point. Can we trust the *source* of the information?

After research found links between sugar consumption and heart health, the sugar lobby in the USA (back then called the Sugar Research Foundation) ended the study and never published the results. Instead, one of the foundation's top executives, John Hickson, secretly paid two influential Harvard scientists to publish a paper shifting the blame to saturated fat.[22] This example shows how important it is to understand what *motivates* your source to put out a certain piece of information. Why go through the effort to say or publish something? What is the motivation of your source? Where does their funding come from? Even more importantly, who benefits from it?

Motivations don't need to be that nefarious: take publication bias in science. It is well documented that scientists tend to publish only articles that show significant positive results.[23] In other words, the outcome of a study determines to some extent its likelihood of publication. This behaviour is completely rational from both the scientist's and the journal's point of view, but leads to a disturbed balance of scientific findings and hence a distorted 'scientific consensus' on important scientific matters.

In addition to the motivation, ask yourself if the source is *able* to deliver a true statement. Is it *capable* of doing the research and analysis necessary to arrive at trustworthy information? Just as you might not trust a drunk person to give you accurate directions when asking for the way, you might not want to go to a spiritual healer with little classical medical education when you've broken your leg.

7. Tap into other people's minds

As we have argued above, we tend to favour one interpretation too early in the process of problem solving and don't change our beliefs when faced with counter-evidence. We accept stories and narrative explanations, but disregard observations that call for alternative interpretations. The solution for this inherent bias is simple: tap into other people's minds for help.

Chances are you deal with other people in your job on a daily basis. Most likely, they will not have the same blind spots as you, as everyone's life path is different. By designating different roles for them to play, you can use their analytical focus deliberately to check beliefs. Here are two specific 'hats' that worked well in team settings:

- **The devil's advocate:** this is a particularly critical team member who, first and foremost, points out the problems and risks of an approach. They do not necessarily disbelieve the proposition, but are focused on testing its validity. They find new evidence that you might not know and might not be motivated to seek out in the first place. A similar exercise is establishing what the CIA and government contractors have termed 'red teams' or 'red cells'. These are independent groups that purposely challenge incumbent opinions or viewpoints in order to detect flaws, blind spots or other shortcomings. The CIA created them in the aftermath of the 9/11 attacks and they have proved to be an influential asset.[24]

- **The fact-checker:** they bring to light hidden assumptions in statements, and double-check facts. As opposed to the devil's advocate, the fact-checker does not necessarily take a position contrary to yours. Their role is simply to dig deeper, surface implicit premises, compare statements with evidence and inject facts into the conversation.

Don't expect people to play these roles organically. Particularly in hierarchical settings, there are few incentives to raise critical points. It is better to deliberately nominate people to fill these roles. You may also think about rotating roles frequently, say for each team meeting. This will not only benefit your job at hand, but also allow those who play the roles to become more attentive, critical thinkers.

//////////////////// THE BOTTOM LINE ////////////////////

Humans don't have a built-in mechanism to detect false beliefs, or to be good at acknowledging what we don't know. Instead, we typically look for evidence to confirm our biases, and make up satisfying stories to fill in the gaps. To be a good problem solver, it is paramount to regularly review your belief system, calibrate confidence levels and actively practise humility.

Chapter Two

Bust your biases

See through the games your brain plays

It is paradoxical yet true to say that the more we know, the more ignorant we become in the absolute sense, for it is only through enlightenment that we become conscious of our limitations. Precisely one of the most gratifying results of intellectual evolution is the continuous opening up of new and greater prospects.
Nikola Tesla

BENEFITS OF THIS MENTAL TACTIC

Systematically surfacing and examining your biases is a way to expand your field of vision – to not only see more clearly but also to see more broadly. This is critical at the evidence-gathering stage. The quality of your analyses and recommendations (outputs) is a function of your inputs (the data and evidence you assemble). Your goal should be to be as objective and comprehensive as possible.

Remember, these are only tendencies. Not everything we talk about here will resonate with you. You might even feel like you *never* do any of these things. While we might politely suggest you're at risk of the overconfidence bias, that's ok. It's an antidote to snap judgements and an aid to thinking clearly about situations and people.

We think this mental tactic will help you when you are in information-hunting mode, processing mode or reflecting mode.

SEE THROUGH THE GAMES YOUR BRAIN PLAYS

Have you ever arrived home at the end of a long day and not been quite sure how you got there? Do you order the same thing over and over again for lunch, even if somewhere in your mind you are aware there is something you might like more if only you could discover it? Have you ever met someone new who looked a bit like a friend of yours and immediately formed a view about what their personality must be like? Even months later, once you realised they were nothing like your friend, did it still take you a while to shake your initial assumptions?

We have talked about how to overcome your blind spots and to detect and change erroneous beliefs. Now we will talk about what happens when you start to gather evidence to update these beliefs. We want to highlight the ways in which our human processing skills are limited, how strongly instinctive reactions drive our decisions and guide you through the predictable biases you might encounter. We will then give you some tools to overcome them.

///////////////////// # COGNITIVE BIASES /////////////////////

In recent decades, psychologists and behavioural economists have uncovered a number of cognitive biases that systematically distort our information-gathering and decision making. The *dual processing theory* argues that human decisions are guided by two separate systems.[25] System 1 is the older system, a hangover from our past as primates, and relies on our intuition. System 2, on the other hand, is guided by reason and thought.[26] You can think of System 1 as the instinctive system and System 2 as the deliberate system.

System 1 thinking is typically much faster, more frequent and automatic, but relies on stereotypes and rough approximations. Our predecessors wouldn't need to know if the blurry object on the horizon was a lion or a rhino. The only important thing was that the fight or flight trigger be pressed. System 1 thinking is a kind of mental autopilot. If you've ever pulled your car into your driveway while lost in thought and been a little startled to find yourself there, System 1 was doing the guiding. System 1 is incredibly useful as it allows us to navigate the world without constantly having to make and re-make decisions, preventing us from becoming totally overwhelmed.

System 2 thinking is often characterised as deliberate, effortful and reflective. We use System 2 thinking, for instance, when trying to form sentences in a language we are just learning, following the directions to assemble IKEA furniture, or making the trade-offs associated with opening the company's new business unit.

Many of the biases that behavioural scientists have uncovered over the last few decades stem from using System 1 thinking in situations that require more thought and reflection – that is, in situations where System 2 might serve us better. In many cases, System 1 thinking narrows our perspective in a way that makes us focus only on one particular aspect of a situation, ignoring all others. Here we're going to explore the ways in which biases can limit our ability to effectively gather information – and how to do better.

Evolution helps – and hurts

As the state of cognitive science, social psychology and research into judgement and decision making expands, we learn ever more about the limitations of human beings as information processors and decision makers. To date, researchers have documented more than a hundred cognitive biases that can impede our judgement. Ironically, it is precisely some of these biases that have allowed human beings to survive as long as we have. The world is a complex place, and there is a great deal of data coming at us all at once. You can think of our biases almost like blinders that help us sort friend from foe, food from poison, threat from opportunity. In the modern world, our information-processing demands are frequently much more complex.

Our goal here is to identify some categories of blinders that are likely to affect you – and all of us – as we make decisions. By definition, this list cannot be complete, but we hope that you will take three things away from this:

- Information-gathering and processing is rooted in our animalistic selves; truth-seeking is secondary to rapid information processing and self-preservation.

- There are a number of predictable biases that will surface again and again as you and your teams attempt to gather information systematically and make sense of it.

- But you can take steps to recognise, reduce and counteract these biases. We will share some of those tools here.

Researchers have now documented more than a hundred cognitive biases.[27] We will introduce those that we consider to be the most important to the evidence-gathering process.

THE 3Ss: SIMPLIFYING, SENSE-MAKING AND STICKING

Here we share a short introduction to several of the biases that you are most likely to see at play in your life and work. Since Part 1 focuses on collecting evidence, we're going to focus only on those that limit your observation at the evidence-gathering stage. Don't worry, some of the others will make an appearance later as we get into the deciding and taking action phases.

As we begin to process information in preparation for making a decision, we typically encounter three types of distortions. We *simplify,* we try to make *sense* of what we are observing and then we *stick* to the view we have formed. Without awareness and training to see through these biases, it's almost impossible to catch them in the moment.

We simplify and stereotype too fast

In some ways, our brains are like sharks, powering through the water in search of prey, biting down immediately on any information that crosses our path. Human beings are gifted information-seekers. But like a hungry shark, we will often bite down on the first piece of data to cross our path, without pausing to examine it closely. Latching on to a single point of data isn't a problem in itself. In fact, it can often be very efficient. The issue is that it tends to colour all other information that we receive: a phenomenon known as anchoring. These single points of evidence are the things we remember and use to make decisions, often at the expense of more robust averages or representative examples.

The broad category of stereotyping includes a number of biases relevant to observation and data collection, such as the 'conjunction fallacy'. Take the original example that Tversky and Kahneman offer in their seminal 1983 paper:

"Linda is 31 years old, single, outspoken and very bright. She majored in philosophy. As a student, she was deeply concerned with issues of discrimination and social justice, and also participated in anti-nuclear demonstrations."

They then go on to ask: "Which of the following two statements is more likely to be true?

1 Linda is a bank teller.

2 Linda is a bank teller and active in the feminist movement[...]"[28]

It turns out that the overwhelming majority of people, when presented with this case, answer #2. This is even true for many statisticians. If you look closer, however, you notice that the likelihood of any two statements combined (A is true *and* B is true) needs to be at least as high as only one of them (A is true). But because Linda's description fitted neatly into our pre-conception of a feminist, we immediately jump at explanation number 2.

Take a look at the left of the following graphic. The *overlap* (shaded area) visualises the probability of Linda being a bank teller *and* a feminist. The overlapping area will always be smaller than (or equal to) the area in the circle 'bank teller'. The story 'Linda is a bank teller and active in the feminist movement' is, from a standpoint of narrative plausibility, much more salient to us. But statistically, the statement 'Linda is a bank teller' is more likely to be true.

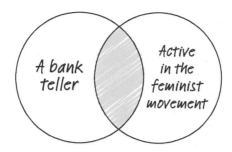

We seek sense and stories even where they don't exist

Just as we have a desire to clutch the first piece of information we see, we also have a tendency to try and make sense of the information we take in as rapidly as possible. As human beings, we have an instinctive desire to tell stories that make sense of the world around us. And we like the stories we tell to be simple, with a strong preference for single-cause explanations. In reality, events almost never have a single cause, but the stories we tell ourselves and each other often do.

Our brains also hold on to these stories much more tightly than we hold on to data. In an informal study, Professor Jennifer Aaker at Stanford University asked her students to recall everything they could about presentations delivered by their fellow students. Just 5% of students could recall the data presented, but a huge 63% of students could recall the stories that were told during the presentations. Aaker told *The Guardian* in a subsequent interview: "Research shows our brains are not hard-wired to understand logic or retain facts for very long. Our brains are wired to understand and retain stories."[29]

This effect can be even stronger when we have a nugget of information to shape our story around. For instance, we often rely on the outcomes of a decision to evaluate its quality or to inform future decisions. A good example of this is when we catch ourselves saying something like: "Sheila turned out to be a really good marketing manager, so our recruiting processes must be good." Using what we know with hindsight to evaluate how we should have decided initially is risky. It does not allow us to correctly weigh random chance or calculated risks.

To see how much we love stories and formulating conclusions, let's look at an experiment by decision scientists Jonathan Baron and John Hershey, who tried to quantify outcome bias. They presented subjects with the case of a 55-year-old man with a heart condition, which could be relieved by a type of bypass operation. But that operation, they told the students, came at a risk as 8% of those undergoing the surgery died. The doctor decided to go ahead with the operation. They told half the subjects that the patient survived the surgery and half the subjects that he died. Subjects were much more likely to declare that the doctor had made the wrong decision when they thought the patient had died.[30]

We stick to the explanations we generate, and it's hard to change our minds

Once we've got hold of some evidence and generated a story around it, it's very difficult for us to move away from it. We love sticking to our stories so much that our brain will hunt for almost any excuse to do so. The term for this is 'confirmation bias' – our tendency to interpret new evidence in light of our existing beliefs or stories.

Confirmation bias affects the way we observe and process a huge range of inputs. For instance, your team has just taken on a new employee, Avery. In the first team meeting, you notice that Avery doesn't say anything and you make a note of this data point. You tell yourself that Avery is a shy, introverted person. In every other encounter, you subconsciously look for evidence that confirms your story: meetings where Avery doesn't speak up, disagreements where she seems reticent, conversations where you feel like she has little to contribute. So powerful is this confirmation bias, that you're likely to forget that second meeting where Avery spoke up more than five times. You may not even register Avery chatting boisterously with colleagues or hosting an energetic discussion with new suppliers.

You've already formed your point of view and your brain is like a heat-seeking missile, looking for information to confirm its conclusions.

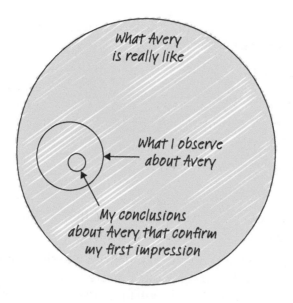

What Avery
is really like

What I observe
about Avery

My conclusions
about Avery that confirm
my first impression

DE-BIAS YOURSELF

Once you understand these games that our brains inevitably play, it's natural to want to play too – to see if you can find a way to overcome your own biases. As you embark on that journey, we ask you to first recognise that System 1 can be valuable in many ways. We simply could not function if we had to carefully weigh and process all of the information coming at us at all times. While System 1 can be incredibly useful, it can also get in the way of thoughtful, objective decision making. It is a valuable goal to ensure that you can interrupt yourself at important moments. We want to share here the approaches to doing this that have been valuable for us.

Be suspicious about yourself

First of all, it is important to realise *when* a bias *could* be at work. As we will say often in this book, mindful awareness of how you're making the decision, and the forces acting on you, is the first step to deciding differently. This kind of situational awareness allows you to earmark or flag situations that could potentially be affected by situational biases. How certain are you about a fact? How firm are you in your belief?

The higher your confidence level, the less likely you are to notice or actively look for evidence that could counter your existing beliefs. For instance, if you're particularly enthusiastic about a company's new product (maybe you even had a hand in creating it), it will be harder for you to listen to criticisms from other divisions, or rationally review market research that suggests people do not like the product.

When we meet new people, we instinctively form a judgement of them. Inevitably, that first impression will be weighted by our brains more heavily than the second, third or tenth impression. Indeed, that first impression will weigh so heavily that it will colour all subsequent impressions. As a starting point, as you go through your day tomorrow, just notice situations where you could be vulnerable to one of the 3Ss.

Look for ways to learn more about your own tendencies and situations where you might be more prone to bias without being consciously aware. One very valuable starting point is Harvard's Implicit Association Test.[31] It will highlight the connections that your brain makes naturally between categories (e.g. are you more likely to associate the word scientist with man or with woman? Are you more likely to associate the word parent with man or with woman?) Taking the tests won't de-bias you, but it will help you notice where to focus.[32]

Deliberately build ways to gather objective evidence

Once you've identified a situation where you might be vulnerable to bias, you need a way to beat your brain at its own game. You need to put in place a way to gather new data and tell different stories. One of the best ways to do this is to deliberately gather objective, comprehensive evidence.

The two of us met during graduate school at Harvard University, where we observed an institution working hard to replace knee-jerk System 1 thinking with rational System 2 thinking. In the Harvard Business School MBA programme, class participation can count for half of a student's final grade.[33] You can easily imagine that in the first week, a professor forms a snap judgement of how often members of the class speak up. You can also envisage that a professor might be very influenced by stereotypes – perhaps by the assumption that men might be more confident or assertive than women.

This is historically what has happened, with men receiving consistently higher-class participation grades than women. As a way to make the class discussion process fairer for all, the business school introduced a tracking system – a scribe sat in the room recording notes on the contribution (or not) of each student. The professor could then refer to this objective record while assigning grades, rather than relying on their own biased impressions and memory.

Deliberately diversify

As you collect evidence, deliberately look for opposing views. You can do this in almost any domain – seeking out media you wouldn't typically consume (perhaps a newspaper or news website), keeping a deliberate tally in meetings of how often your timid team member speaks up in weekly meetings. In our personal lives, we ask friends who hold very different political views to suggest reading materials or commentators that we might like to follow on Twitter. We do the same with our friends from different parts of the world. It's easy for Julia to be well-informed about the latest developments in Australian politics, for example, but she needs some nudges to pay attention to news from Southern Europe.

/////////////////////////// CHECKLIST ///////////////////////////

How to de-bias yourself

 CHECK YOURSELF BEFORE YOU WRECK YOURSELF

As we encouraged you before, adapt a sceptic's mindset – even towards yourself. It is healthy to start from the assumption that your frame of reference is limited and to look for ways to expand it.

 BUILD AN OBJECTIVE EVIDENCE BASE

When the decision really matters, start with the goal of systematically gathering evidence to answer the question, rather than relying on your own impressions. Be able to answer the question: "What would make you change your mind?"

 MANAGE INCOMING MESSAGES

Seek ways to diversify your inputs right now. Don't wait until you are trying to solve a really difficult problem to do this, open yourself up to new perspectives as a matter of course.

/////////////////////////// THE BOTTOM LINE ///////////////////////////

Our minds use a lot of shortcuts to help us navigate the world. The problem is that most of these shortcuts are adapted for an environment that is long gone, and lead to biases in modern social settings. As far as gathering data and evidence is concerned, three types of biases are particularly relevant. First, simplification and stereotyping. Second, accepting stories that seem to make sense too quickly. Third, the inherent stickiness of the beliefs we hold. Actively de-biasing yourself takes time, but can be learned. It all starts with acknowledging the various distortions, being mindful and aware, as well as practising ways to deliberately shift down into System 2.

Chapter Three

Explore your data

Gather, scrutinise and visualise information to discover insights

The goal is to turn data into information, and information into insight.

Carly Fiorina, former CEO of Hewlett-Packard Co

BENEFITS OF THIS MENTAL TACTIC

When we first set out to examine or resolve a problem, we naturally start to look for evidence. When we do, we often jump at the first clue. This is misdirected – if your data does not do a reasonable job of reflecting reality, you risk missing the point entirely.

We are often consumers of data, rather than direct producers of analysis. You are typically critically examining someone's output, rather than compiling it yourself. So the checklist looks a little different – it's a guide to what questions to ask and when.

GATHER, SCRUTINISE AND VISUALISE INFORMATION TO DISCOVER INSIGHTS

When should you start a company?

There is a pervasive belief in Silicon Valley that the best technology CEOs are the youngest. They are capable of the most original ideas, can disrupt existing industries and are prepared to take the biggest risks. Pause for a moment and imagine a successful technology CEO. What do they look like? I bet they're wearing jeans and sneakers, and they are young. Very young. This is an extremely common assumption. So common, in fact, that major investors and venture capitalists have started to look with some suspicion upon CEOs older than about 30. Paul Graham, co-founder of leading incubator Y-Combinator, told *The New York Times*: "The cut-off in investors' heads is 32."[34]

Is this what a CEO
looks like?

This assumption makes some sense. We can all readily summon an image of a superstar founder like Mark Zuckerberg, who founded Facebook from his Harvard dorm room, or Sergey Brin, who co-founded Google at 25. The problem with drawing inferences from these readily accessible data points is that they turn out to be totally unrepresentative and easily refuted by data. Here we will illuminate why we often struggle to use quantitative evidence to make persuasive arguments.

We will return to our CEO friends in a moment. First, we want to give you the tools to gather data correctly – and make sense of it. These tools will help you to overcome the biases we have just discussed, opening the way for more rational and objective decision making.

One of the first steps in making consistent, high-quality decisions is getting access to, and using, the data that will help you formulate an objective point of view. Many of us think that we have a good handle on how to access, manipulate and make sense of data. The evidence suggests otherwise: we don't think clearly and carefully about problems, even when lots of money is on the line. We don't design structured, data-driven approaches to solving problems, even when we could. As Paul Graham put it in the same interview: "I can be tricked by anyone who looks like Mark Zuckerberg."[35]

Back to the CEOs. It turns out that the wildly successful young CEO is a myth. Here's where four talented, quantitatively minded researchers come in: Pierre Azoulay, Benjamin Jones, J. Daniel Kim and Javier Miranda. They'd also looked around at the magazine covers trumpeting CEOs in their twenties or start-up founders in their teens. After examining the winners of a prominent start-up competition, they concluded that the winners were, on average, 29.[36] The judges of this competition are savvy, sophisticated investors, who must know what they are doing. Wrong.

Using data from the United States Census Bureau, the researchers examined the average age at which Americans founded a business. It turned out that the *average* age for starting a business was 42 – more than double the age of 19-year-old Facebook founder Zuckerberg. Furthermore, the researchers found that older entrepreneurs were more likely to succeed beyond their wildest imaginations. Extreme start-up success (defined by being in the top 0.1% of start-ups by employment growth) increased as entrepreneurs aged, all the way until their late fifties. Our entrepreneurial heroes, it turns out, don't look anything like Mark Zuckerberg. We want to help you stop thinking in terms of single data points (whether one outlier or an average) and start thinking in terms of distributions.

FORMULATE YOUR HYPOTHESIS

Sometimes you'll be handed a pile of data, such as a quarterly sales report, a bundle of receipts, a list of the GDP growth rates of various countries, and asked to make sense of it. You also might be the one handing someone the data and will then need to check if someone *has* indeed made sense of it.

To start the process of sense-making, you need to be systematic. As a first step, we urge you to lay out a hypothesis, and use that as the basis for checking your work. Without a hypothesis, you can play around in the data forever without ever really making progress.[37]

You should think about data analysis as the opportunity to generate insight into one or more very specific questions. The best entry point for that type of exercise is to state a clear hypothesis, which is framed in the form of a proposition, not a question. Imagine that you have some annual sales data about your sales people, some of whom receive an incentive payment for bringing in additional business and others who just receive their fixed salary. You are curious about whether the incentive payment is worthwhile and jot down some ingoing hypotheses (think of these as *very* early thoughts). A quick list might look something like this.

H1: Sales people sell more when offered an incentive payment

H2: Sales increase in line with an increasing rate of potential incentive payment

H3: The resulting increased sales outweigh the cost of providing the incentive payment

Sometimes when we mentor new or junior staff, they are hesitant to commit to a hypothesis. They are fearful that if the hypothesis is disproven, this will somehow reflect badly on them. We may hear something like: "I don't want to venture an opinion until I have looked at the data thoroughly" or "It's too soon to say anything." We understand, but a hypothesis is a proposition, not an answer or a conclusion. The purpose of stating your hypothesis is to structure and prioritise your analysis. Without it, you could be swimming in data forever. This step is even more important if you won't be the one performing the analysis, but are the end-consumer. If someone on your team or an advisor is preparing to do this work, it's critical that you are involved in formulating and refining your hypotheses so that you get what you want from the exercise.

SCRUTINISE YOUR DATA

Even though you've developed a number of thoughtful hypotheses, don't jump right into testing them just yet. You first need to check if your data is actually suitable for that job. The following checklist provides an overview of the questions we typically ask before diving into data sets.

WHAT TO ASK	WHY IT MATTERS	EXAMPLE
Is this data set fully representative?	Your data needs to approximate reality. It can do that in one of two ways: ● whole population data ● random samples. If your data does not comprise the whole population of observations or a statistical random sample, it will not be representative. This means it will be not be possible to draw statistically valid inferences from the data. It *may* still provide helpful insights into the issue that you are wrestling with, but you should be wary.	You might have data on every single transaction every customer has ever performed with your company. For your purposes, that can be considered population data. But if, for instance, you only had a record of credit card, but not cash transactions, that would not be representative. Sometimes it's unwieldy, impractical or expensive to try and gather data on a whole population. For example, say you wanted to understand the satisfaction of every employee in the organisation. You *could* ask every individual or you could ask a random sample of the same employees. The important thing is that the sample approximates your population on dimensions that matter (it has about the same number of women and men as in your total labour pool, representative numbers of older and younger people, and a sample of people from all locations).

→

WHAT TO ASK	WHY IT MATTERS	EXAMPLE
What are the sources of this data set? How was it collected?	Warning signs of data that is likely to be biased or unrepresentative: ● Self-selected responses: is there any particular sub-group of people who are more likely than others to respond? ● Self-reported responses: people have a tendency to answer questions in a way that will be seen favourably by others. ● Self-interested analyst: data where the person conducting the research has an interest in the outcome should also be viewed with suspicion. For instance, a study by a cleaning products manufacturer that concludes that the average home is filled with harmful bacteria that can be removed with vigorous use of cleaning products should be treated with suspicion. ● Intentional responses versus observed behaviors: asking gym members if they intend to exercise during next week is likely to be much less indicative of actual exercise habits than reviewing the logs of members signing into the gym itself (revealed preferences).	Continuing our employee survey example, if you send out a survey to all your employees asking about their satisfaction, you should assume that your responses are representative. Who replies to such surveys? Those who are very satisfied, those who are very dissatisfied, and those who have an interest in the results looking particularly strong or weak. Second, if you are asking people what they do versus observing what they do or have done, be warned. As a behavioural economist, one of the axioms Julia lives by is "everyone misleads, without bad intent". People will tend to overstate their positive behaviours and understate their less-positive ones (this is called the 'self-serving bias'). Anytime you are relying on self-reported data, you should be looking for risks of self-serving bias. For example, if you ask members of heterosexual couples what percentage of the housework each of them does, the total will typically add to much more than 100%. Clearly, observing behaviour or even reviewing household labour diaries here would be much more valuable.

WHAT TO ASK	WHY IT MATTERS	EXAMPLE
Who is *not* captured in this data set?[38]	Knowing who or what is missing from your data set is critically important. There are two failure modes to be aware of: • Data missing at random: think of this as observations that have been excluded from your data set but not in a way that influences the variables you are interested in. • Data missing not at random: observations that are missing from your data set in ways that *do* affect the variables you are interested in. These are systematic biases that will distort the insights you may be able to extract from the data set significantly.	What do these two types of missing data look like? • Data missing at random: say the point-of-sale machine wasn't accurately recording transactions in one of your stores one day in May. For that store, you only have 364 days of data. Unless that day is particularly important to the analysis (e.g. the shopping holiday Black Friday), its exclusion probably doesn't alter your analysis of which stores are most successful. You might be able to supplement this missing data by including the data from the same day in the same store a year prior. • Data missing not at random: in our sales data set, online sales in certain states are not captured, only direct sales made by human sales people, as well as online sales in other states. In this case, you need to find a different way to gather the missing data before proceeding. Or you can use it to reach conclusions about your human sales people, but not your online channels.

PUT YOUR DATA IN THE BIN

So you've reviewed the table on the previous pages and are comfortable with your data. It seems representative, relatively unbiased and fit for purpose. Now let's put it to good use.

Our brains love what economists call 'reference points'. These are bits of data that we can latch on to and start to organise our thoughts around. An average is a classic reference point. We all recall from school maths that an average is calculated by dividing the sum of all the values in the set by their number. In that sense, the average is useful. It lets us get an idea of what is about right.

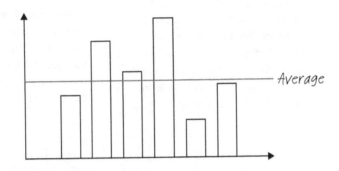

But in another sense, an average is almost no help at all, and the fixation that executives, educators, politicians and analysts have on average performance can be misleading and even dangerous. On the other hand, averages can be an extremely powerful motivational tool. Human beings love comparing themselves to the average and trying to beat it.

As a starting point, let's consider the example of a biology teacher with a class of 30 students. These students are regularly tested with written exams to determine their understanding of the course material. Of course, some students perform better than others. Here's a simple plot of their performance on the last exam: the number of students with a particular score on the Y-axis, and the score (out of 100) on the X-axis.

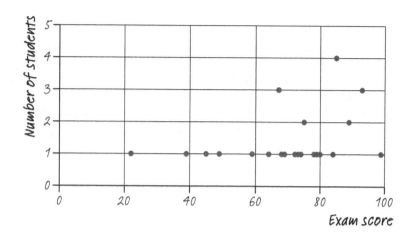

We can start to make some observations about how our data is distributed. We have a small number of students scoring less than 50 out of 100, quite a large number scoring between 60 and 80 and a sizeable amount scoring between 80 and 100. To really make sense of any new data set, the first thing we do is put it into a histogram. We think the histogram is a vital but unloved graph. A histogram immediately lets you start to explore probabilities. It gives you an opportunity to visualise how likely a certain observation (in this case, a score) is.

Check out the histogram for these test scores.

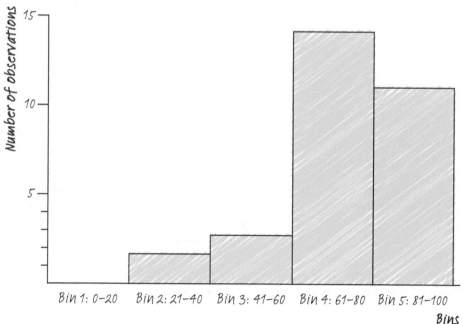

Once we have this histogram, we can immediately examine over and underperformance. We can also start to see how the data is distributed. See below for a rough sketch of the data distribution here. You have a class who performed pretty well on this test, but with some clear under-performers. Imagine repeating this exercise for sales people and revenue generation, or IT support teams and number of requests processed. You can immediately see the power of the histogram in shaping our impressions of data. We can see a good number of students performing very well on the test, a large number performing well and a smaller number (the 'tail' struggling).

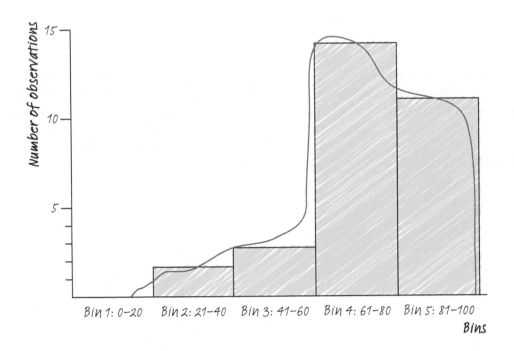

From looking at the above, you should have the impression that an average (mean) score is not necessarily terribly useful here. But there are a few other scores you might find helpful to know. You might want to understand the range of performance by looking at the minimum and maximum scores. After we've plotted our histogram, we immediately run a set of descriptive statistics to help us investigate the story the data is telling. We're going to do exactly that for this data set on the following page. The goal of all of this work is to help you get a sense of the data, not necessarily to reach any conclusions. For example, we don't know from the above histogram whether the test was difficult or easy, whether the worse-performing students were confused or ill or just distracted after lunch. Once you have your histogram, the next step should be a 'five-number summary'.

USING DESCRIPTIVE STATISTICS

The five-number summary is a simple tool to help you explore your data one step further. For this data set, it looks like this.

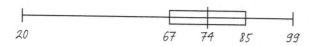

The diagram is known as a 'box and whiskers' plot. It's another under-rated graph, and powerfully visualises your data. In a box and whiskers plot, five things are on display:

- The median, or the score at the midpoint of your distribution. It's always helpful to take the median of a dataset as well as the average, since it's less sensitive to outlier values (e.g. a very high or a very low score).

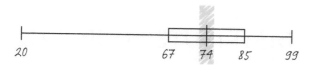

- The minimum observation in the data set (in this case, our unfortunate student scoring 20).

- The maximum observation in the data set (in this case, our 99% smarty-pants).

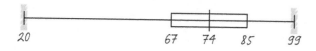

- The first quartile of the data set (Q1) and the third quartile in the data set (in this case 67 and 85, respectively).

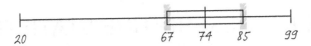

The data exercises we've just described take almost no time. In a small data set, you can perform them by hand like we did here. In a large data set, data analysis packages (Microsoft Excel, SPSS, Stata, R) will allow you to compute them almost instantly. For those of you who manage people who do the data analysis, asking for these quick descriptive overviews before any other work starts gives you a reality check on the data that you are working with.

These three tools (x–y scatter plot, histograms and box and whiskers plots) can be a powerful help in getting to grips with your data. Imagine for a moment that you are a call centre manager and that the data we used above represents the average minutes of idle time each of your staff has between calls. It is now very easy to identify leaders and laggards and see the variation in performance among your team. In our box and whiskers plot, our teacher has immediately segmented his data. No longer does he have 30 students, but 4 clusters of performers who might each require a different approach.

DISTRIBUTE YOUR DATA

Now that you've seen how values in one example are distributed, we want to introduce you to some common distributions (that is, the shapes that our data can take), and to help you anticipate where you might see them.[39] By knowing the most common types of distributions and the conditions under which they are most likely to occur, you can make inferences about the likelihood of having observed what you, in fact, *did* observe. Even more importantly, knowing the typical distributions will help you make a better guess about those data points you haven't yet observed. Understanding the distribution of your data is how you move beyond single observations to identifying patterns.

Normal distribution

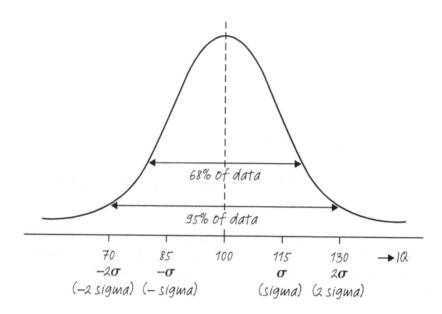

This is the distribution you are most likely to be familiar with (commonly called the 'bell curve' for its shape, or also the Gaussian curve after the famous mathematician and physicist Carl Friedrich Gauss). It's one of the most prevalent distributions that occur in natural history. For example, distribution of human heights or IQs typically take the form of a bell curve. The mean IQ of the population is standardised at 100. This means you can expect 68% of the population to have IQs between 85 and 115, and 95% between 70 and 130. In other words, it's extremely unlikely for a randomly picked person to have an IQ above 130 or below 70.

Pareto distribution

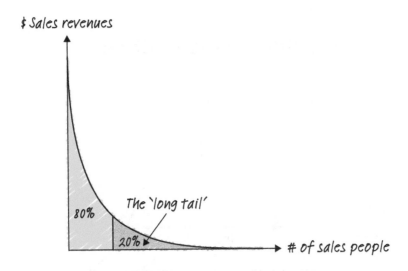

You might have heard of the 80:20 rule. It's the idea that 80% of the sales are made by 20% of the sales people or that 80% of the complaints are caused by 20% of customers. This broad phenomenon is captured by the pareto principle. When you see a distribution like this, you're seeing a story where a relatively small number of the inputs are responsible for a relatively large share of the output.

Where can you see this distribution in action? Many communities (especially online – think of Wikipedia or YouTube) are powered by super-users. Super-users are individuals who spend much of their personal time and energy on a platform. Your super-users are your outliers in that they sit outside (sometimes very far outside) the two standard deviations described above. But their impact can be disproportionate.

For instance, in 2015, the well-known blog Priceonomics reported that Wikipedia had some serious outliers: "Of Wikipedia's 26 million registered users, roughly 125,000 (less than 0.5%) are 'active' editors. Of these 125,000, only some 12,000 have made more than 50 edits over the past six months."[40]

As you think about your average customer, you should also ask yourself, who are your power-users and what do they contribute? How well are you serving or appreciating these statistical outliers? Does the change you are contemplating work for them?

Poisson distribution

Whenever you estimate the number of events per unit of time, area or volume, you will be using the Poisson distribution. One of the first real-world datasets that contained a Poisson distribution was a list of Prussian soldiers accidentally killed by a horse-kick between 1875 and 1894. Other examples include the arrivals of customers in a retail store per hour, the number of customers who call about a problem per month or the number of aeroplane crashes per one million flight hours.

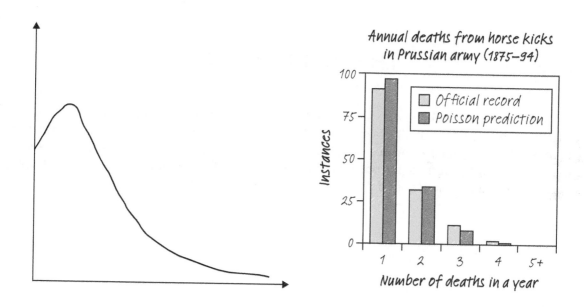

Annual deaths from horse kicks in Prussian army (1875–94)

Official record
Poisson prediction

Instances

Number of deaths in a year

Uniform distribution

The uniform (also called rectangular) distribution is the simplest of all distributions. Typical examples are the serial number on a randomly selected dollar note, or the number that comes up when you roll a fair dice or when you spin a roulette wheel.

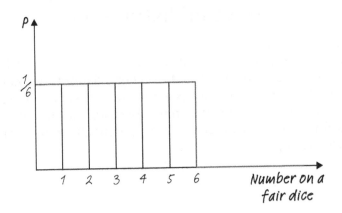

/////////////////// THE BOTTOM LINE ///////////////////

The data you use to kick off your analysis will determine how useful your results are – and whether they are useful at all. Make sure that your data is good quality, and form hypotheses to make sense of your information. Always look for ways to go beyond the average and see the full picture of your data (by looking at descriptive statistics and forming views about the underlying distribution of your data). That's where the real insight is.

Part 2

Connect the dots

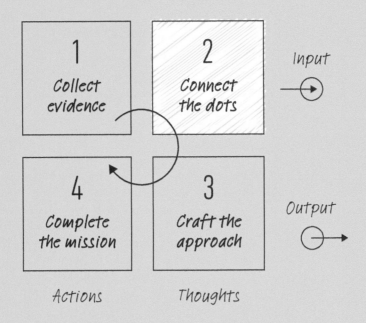

1	2
Collect evidence	Connect the dots
4	3
Complete the mission	Craft the approach

Actions Thoughts

Input →⊕

Output ⊖→

Part 1 of this book revealed the distortions, distractions and biases that affect us when we handle data. Our brains are adapted to make quick-fire decisions in the fight or flight environments of thousands of years ago, not in the businesses and boardrooms of today. Mental glitches are frequently the consequence. Part 1 provided tools to make you a more proactive perceiver. You are now able to observe facts more clearly, source information in an unbiased way and turn your attention to what's not obvious. Equipped with mental tactics that help shed light on the unknown and uncertain, you're now ready for the next step.

Humans love to speculate about how things work and why they go wrong. It's a natural impulse that's also the cornerstone of critical thinking. Welcome to Part 2 of *The Decision Maker's Playbook*: Connect the dots.

In this part, we provide mental tactics to analyse the data that has been collected.

First, we will introduce tree diagrams as a method of breaking a structure into its components and identify the real root causes of problems.

Second, we will analyse how randomness can confuse our clear thinking about causal relationships. In our attempt to isolate distinct causal links, chance can get in the way. This mental tactic can help you to see clearly.

Last, having distinguished skill from luck (or real causality from randomness), we will take a look at more complex systems of causal relationships. 'Thinking in systems' is a mental tactic that will allow you to connect causal influences (such as word-of-mouth and advertising) to outcomes (such as unit sales). Systems thinking explains dynamics such as population growth or hyperinflations and is a useful tool to uncover solutions for a broad variety of problems, including climate change, healthcare and personal wealth management.

Chapter Four

Drill down

Use tree diagrams to deconstruct any problem

The only people who see the whole picture are the ones who step outside the frame.

Salman Rushdie, *The Ground Beneath Her Feet*

BENEFITS OF THIS MENTAL TACTIC

Breaking data down into its components helps you structure projects, find important sources of value and identify root causes. Tree diagrams have stood the test of time to be the key visualisation tools for this. They prompt you to think through the relationships between parts and help you with communicating complex matters. They enable you to ask more useful questions such as "Is what I'm observing an extreme case, or average?" and form hypotheses about the rest of the population in a sample. As a result, they can help find value that would have remained hidden.

Tree diagrams are a useful tool when:

- understanding the drivers of cost and revenue for a business
- designing a work plan for a project
- identifying the failure modes of a product or software
- hypothesising about root causes
- diagnosing a disease, given symptoms
- understanding and influencing value drivers (revenues, profits, costs)
- prioritising components of a problem to solve
- thinking through arguments logically, assessing necessary and sufficient conditions
- visualising multi-stage outcomes and product variations
- mapping out probabilities.

USE TREE DIAGRAMS TO DECONSTRUCT ANY PROBLEM

Let's say you've taken stock of your cognitive inventory. You've thought hard about the legitimacy of the beliefs you hold, and you are ready to uncover any potential blind spots. You have taken into account any cognitive biases that distort your clear thinking, and you've learned about the conditions required for data to be trustworthy, such as sample size and representativeness.

Now it is time to analyse your dataset: to peel back the layers of the onion. The primary way to do so is through tree diagrams.

Tree diagrams (or driver trees as they are sometimes known) help break down complex problems into their individual parts, equations into their factors and goals into their components. They also come in handy if you are trying to categorise or segment a market or customer type. Trees are the manager's favourite tool to graphically structure thinking. Just as a tree is made up of multiple levels – a trunk, branches, twigs and leaves – the visual tree diagram has similar features.

By their nature, tree diagrams prompt you to be comprehensive. They capture all of the components that make up the issue being investigated. Trees allow you to zero in on the factors that are or could be responsible for the behaviour (or outcome) you observe. For example, let's say you stroll outside your home one morning and your car won't start. There could be myriad causes. A tree diagram won't get your car started again but it might help you figure out what's going wrong.

Developed in 1962 by H.A. Watson of Bell Labs, the tree diagram found its initial use as a *fault tree*. Fault trees visualise failure paths within a system and make it easy to find problems, test reliability and assess safety.

Let's look at an example of a fault tree: identifying the reasons for your car not starting. What could be the potential reasons for the car's inability to start? First-level branches divide the problem into user, mechanical and electrical errors. On the second level, each of those categories further divide into a number of separate reasons.

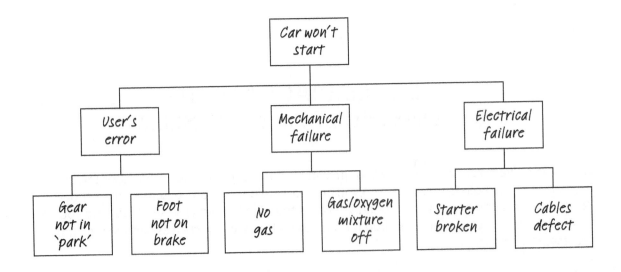

CLARIFYING PRIORITIES FOR FURTHER ANALYSIS

Let's start with an example from the financial world. In typical business situations you are interested in the key drivers to increase or decrease a particular value, say revenues or costs.

Here's a simple driver tree that adds up costs for a fictional airline, Dhar Airways.

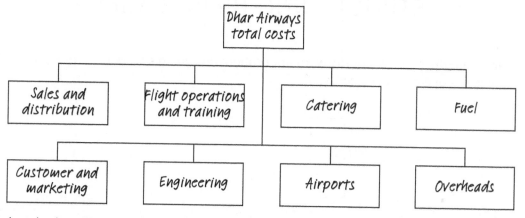

Or take a look at the driver tree below which focuses on website traffic and generated revenues. Note that this tree could have been designed in a more complex way, depending on the question you are trying to answer.

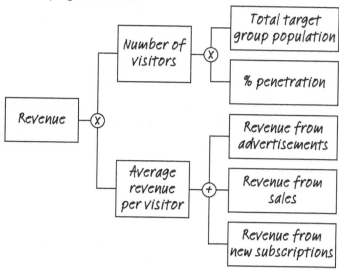

Trees like the one illustrated can help you distinguish important and irrelevant drivers as well as point you towards the factors that are most likely to cause the effect you are interested in (in this case, revenues). They also help you understand where the opportunity lies. It could be that you've only reached a tiny number of your target group (revealed by % penetration) or it could be that revenue from advertisements is quite high, but from sales is tiny.

STRUCTURING HIERARCHIES

Let's start with the most straightforward application: designing a work plan for a project. The different levels of a project could be:

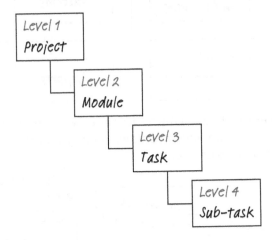

The completion of all work packages is necessary for a task to be completed. The completion of all tasks is necessary for a module to be completed, and so on.

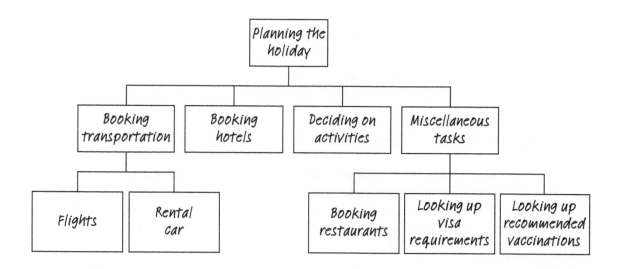

As a graphic way of depicting hierarchies, tree diagrams are also widely used for depicting organisational charts or structures of departments and offices.

///////////////////////// CHECKLIST /////////////////////////

How to plant a tree

 ## DECIDE ON VERTICAL OR HORIZONTAL LAYOUT

Trees are typically built from top to bottom or from left to right. Except for space limitations on the paper in front of you, there are no rules as to what layout to use. We tend to use top-to-bottom trees for breakdowns of modules, products or failure modes. For breakdowns of quantitative structure or causal relationships, we typically use left-to-right tree charts.

 ## SKETCH OUT THE TREE

Start by writing the theme or question at the top (or left) of the diagram. Create the first sub-level of branches by asking yourself which factors add up to whatever you wrote at the top.

 ## VERIFY THAT THE TREE IS MECE – NO OVERLAPS, NO GAPS

You might have heard of the abbreviation MECE (pronounced mee cee). It stands for mutually exclusive, collectively exhaustive. It is a helpful framework to break down a bigger issue into its parts. First, the elements of the sub-level must be *distinct* from each other. There shouldn't be any overlap. This forces you to carefully look at each box on the sub-level and make sure you haven't accidently put parts in more than one box. Second, taken together, the total sum of the elements should be *sufficient* to constitute the higher level. When using a tree to display the five team members of a project group, no one should be left out. The problem or structure should be divided into categories with a *finite* number of general categories (boxes on the sub-level).

DEFINE THE FUNCTIONAL DEPENDENCIES

Typically, the functional relationship between any sub-group and the top is 'and'. For example, if the top box says Revenues in North America, the boxes below should say USA, Canada and Mexico. The implicit relationship between them is 'and'.

But it can also be 'or'. For example, for Who murdered Elizabeth? it could be The Gardener or Sir Thomas or Miss Lilly (of course, it could have also been a plot of two or more).

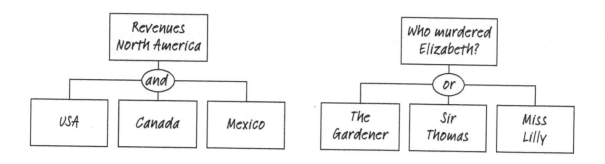

 DECIDE ON AN ADEQUATE LEVEL OF DEPTH, THEN STOP

Trees can extend over a large number of sub-levels. Typically, trees with a level of three or a maximum of four sub-levels are sufficient to visualise and analyse a problem.

Using trees to de-average

We use averages all the time. There are more than 152 sunny days per year in Seattle. The current life expectancy in Japan is 83.8 years. In 2017, more than 40% of the world's population owned a smartphone.

There's nothing wrong with these numbers, but real insights can typically only be gained by breaking down those numbers. As we discussed earlier, averages are a great way to communicate findings but not necessarily an ideal way to truly understand a phenomenon.

Healthcare is one sector where de-averaging is key. Consider Jonathan, Head of Research of a mid-sized company producing dietary supplements. His product development team ran a six-month study to test the efficacy of an all-natural product aimed at lowering blood pressure. The test wasn't able to show positive effects for the average patient. Instead of simply dismissing the product based on the unsuccessful trial, Jonathan's team 'de-averaged' the study results. They discovered that while not all patients responded positively to the blood pressure supplement, a sizeable number of patients did. By de-averaging by age and gender, he found that men under 40 seemed to benefit most. Armed with this knowledge, the product development team brainstormed ways to reach exactly this segment. This way, they avoided blanketing the market with advertising, as doing so would not only be a waste of expenses, but could potentially even lead to negative word-of-mouth and poor reviews from those whom the supplement didn't help.

CHECKLIST

How to de-average

 START WITH WHAT YOU ALREADY KNOW – THE AVERAGE NUMBER

In the following example, the mean income per household is of interest.

Mean income per household, USA (2007), in US$,000	88

 HYPOTHESISE ABOUT RELEVANT AND INTERESTING SUB-SEGMENTS

What are you looking for? Let's say, of particular interest here is the distribution of income by group or percentile of people. This is a common way to look at inequality in a country. Say you are specifically interested in the income distribution of deciles in the population, i.e. 'buckets' of 20% of the whole population. You are particularly keen to know the income of the top 1%. As such, your tree will have six branches.

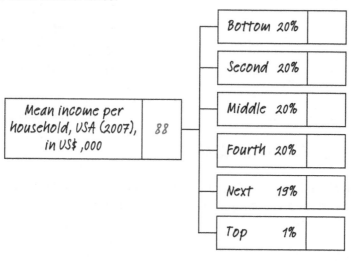

AGGREGATE THE NUMBER

You need to know two variables:

1. The average income for each of the groups

2. The 'weight' of each of the groups

By definition, we already know the weight: it is equivalent to the number of people in each of the branches (the percentage figures in the boxes below). To identify the average income per sub-group, we need to do some research. A good source are international organisations (OECD), universities or research institutes.

The de-averaged mean income per household, broken down into the sub-groups of interest is shown below.

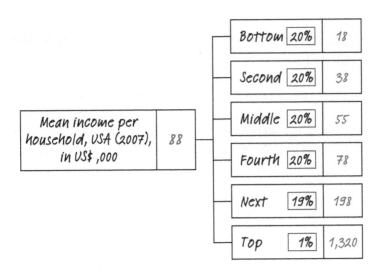

 # DOUBLE-CHECK THE NUMBERS

To do a double-check multiply each weight with the mean income for that sub-group, and add them all up. They need to total the mean income per household.

USING TREES AND FLOW CHARTS TO IDENTIFY A ROOT CAUSE

Trees are a visual tool that breaks an observed phenomenon down into its parts. But they are also suitable for identifying the *root causes* of problems. Root causes are the *ultimate reason* for the existence of a problem. They need to be distinguished from *symptoms* which are simply signals or indicators of the problem. Alleviating symptoms will not affect the root cause. Without tackling the root cause directly, similar symptoms will arise in the future. Let's look at a medical example: a symptom could be a sore throat, a cough or a runny nose. The actual root cause might be an infection. Treating the symptoms will help the patient feel better in the short term: an aspirin will typically reduce these uncomfortable symptoms, but will do nothing to fight the problem's root cause, or in this case cure the illness.

Enter root cause analysis, also known as the 'five-why-analysis' or a cause map. The root cause analysis combines visual thinking with the structured approach of asking "Why?" repeatedly. Here's a simple linear example, analysing the root causes for a student having received a bad grade.

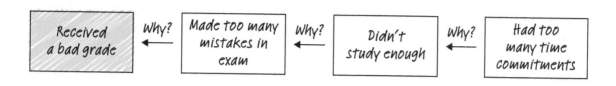

CHECKLIST

Finding root causes

✓ CLEARLY DEFINE THE PROBLEM

Refer to Chapter Zero for more information. Start by writing down the issue or problem in the box to the very left. The empty black boxes will each become building blocks of the analysis.

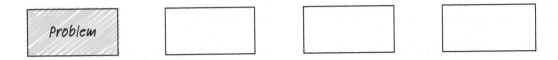

✓ WRITE DOWN THE CAUSES

Then proceed with writing down the causes for each of the previous effects, constantly asking why it happened as you proceed with filling out the boxes on the right.

Connect each of the boxes with an arrow. The arrow has two different meanings:

- From left to right, the arrow prompts the question why this effect happened.
- From right to left, you can substitute the arrow with 'was caused by'.

OBSERVE THE CAUSES

As you continue with the analysis, you will notice that, many times, the causal mesh isn't as linear as in the example shown. Instead, effects can have *multiple* causes in one of the following two ways:

- Both causes were required to bring about the effect (*and*).

- *Either* cause was required to bring about the effect (*or*).

Here's a simple example. To start a fire, you need fuel (tinder, wood, petrol) *and* an initial spark or a flame. But to stop a fire, you can *either* withdraw fuel *or* oxygen.

Using logical operators such as *or* and *and* is closely related to the concept of necessary versus sufficient conditions.

- **Necessary conditions:** we can talk of fuel (tinder) *and* the fire source (spark) as each being *necessary* for the fire to start. Only both of them taken *together* are *sufficient* for the fire.

- **Sufficient conditions:** for the fire to stop, *each* of the displayed reasons in itself is *sufficient*. Either you withdraw the fuel *or* the oxygen – you don't have to do both to stop the fire.

Identifying and working towards fixing the root causes, instead of focusing on the symptoms or first-order effects allows you to tackle problems more effectively and sustainably.

FURTHER EXAMPLES

Optimising your recruiting pipeline

Running a young but growing start-up, Alyssa's first priority is to increase the size of her team with skilled and ambitious talent. Let's say she needs to hire 20 developers over the course of the next month. She's already pulled a number of levers to market the open positions. She has posted on online job boards, social networks such as LinkedIn and local blackboards frequented by developers in areas such as campus cafeterias. And it worked – she has received a number of applications, with varying quality. Using a tree diagram, Alyssa de-averaged the stream of applications and broke them down by channels. To do this, she asked every applicant invited to an interview to fill out a short survey. This allowed her to identify the channels with particularly high-quality applicants, and double-down on those.

THE BOTTOM LINE

Problems and data are often complex and messy. Tree diagrams provide a useful way to add structure to your thinking and give you a useful means of communication. Trees help you break down a trend or dynamic into their drivers, de-average aggregated numbers, find the root cause of a problem, or structure a presentation, project or vacation. Tree diagrams require you to think MECE (mutually exclusive, collectively exhaustive), and allow you to understand problems and data in a much deeper and clearer way.

Chapter Five

Move the needle

Anticipate regression to the mean

The universe is change; our life is what our thoughts make it.[41]

BENEFITS OF THIS MENTAL TACTIC

Understanding regression to the mean will remind you that most outcomes stem from skill and luck.[42] It will encourage you to try and figure out how much of each played a role in a particular outcome. This is important for a number of reasons.

1

It helps assess your outcomes

When skill is involved, a relatively small sample size is sufficient to judge the person or process that lead to an outcome (take chess, for example, which is hard to win by being just lucky). But if more luck is involved, then you will have to look at a much larger group.

2

It allows you to forecast results

Once you know the relative contributions of skill versus luck in a given outcome, it is easier to forecast subsequent outcomes.

3

It helps you calibrate your feedback

Most people agree that praising (or blaming) a person whose success stems only from luck doesn't make sense. With people who are struggling with failure, you can be more helpful by identifying skills they're lacking which, if strengthened, could help them become more successful in the future.

Use this mental tactic whenever you suspect randomness is at play to influence the decision situation at hand.

ANTICIPATE REGRESSION TO THE MEAN

In baseball, the Sophomore Jinx is well known: a player who has a great rookie season is unlikely to do as well or better his second year. That is regression to the mean at work.

In baseball, the best rookie player in each league receives the Rookie of the Year (ROY) Award. But the performance of the winners in their next seasons tends to be worse than in their first year. The rookie fails to live up to the standards of their first effort. Professional athletes aren't the only ones affected by this seeming curse. In the USA, high school and college students who earn the highest grades in their freshman year tend to prove less successful in their second year. And singers and bands who score a big hit with their first album tend to see lower sales of their second album.

So, what's going on? The culprit is regression to the mean, a statistical maxim stating that exceptional outputs tend to decline (regress) to an average over time.

When it comes to human performance, regression to the mean occurs because success is always a function of *both* skill and luck. ROYs, star first-year students and new entertainers who hit it big with their first effort, are always identified as successes on the basis of their exceptional performance.

Since most people assume that performance is based on skill, few of us factor in the role of luck in these early successes – and in later experiences. When performance inevitably regresses to the mean over time, people are surprised and even disillusioned. They don't understand what's required to sustain success or to become successful. In short, people give too much weight to extremes.

AN INTRIGUING DISCOVERY

On 16 February 1822, one of the world's most famous statisticians, Francis Galton, was born. A cousin to Charles Darwin, he came from a very talented family, although he never quite achieved the same level of fame that Darwin did. Still, Galton's achievements were first-rate and his influence on statistics is still felt to this day (he coined the terms correlation, quartile and percentile).

Galton was particularly fascinated by the study of human populations. He was especially devoted to the study of the concept of heredity, how traits were passed from parents to their offspring. Galton first introduced the idea of regression, which meant something completely different from what it stands for today. Instead of typical regression downwards, he meant 'regression to the mean.'

As part of his research, Galton explored the link between heights of parents and their children. He indicated the heights of 928 adult children on one axis and the mid-parent height (average height of father and mother) on the other axis.[43] The result is the chart below.

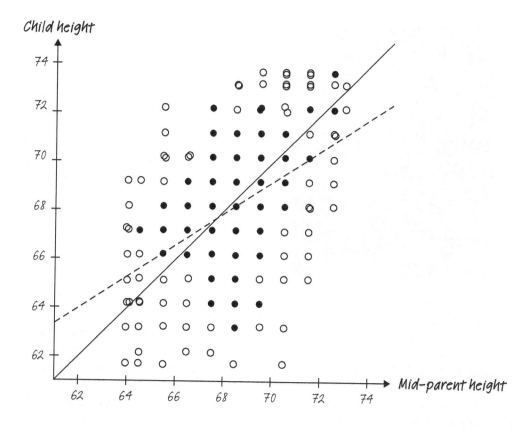

When Galton examined this plot, he expected to see offspring resembling their parents in size. In other words, he expected most points to lie on or near the 45-degree line, which indicate similar heights for parents and their children. But instead, he found that, with parents who were unusually tall, the offspring tended to be shorter than their mother and father, and, with parents who were shorter than usual, many of the offspring were taller.

The data that he collected didn't fit the 45-degree line (solid black in the chart), but rather the slightly less steep dashed line. This suggests that children from exceptionally tall parents are typically *smaller* than them, and children from exceptionally small partners are typically *taller* than them. Galton observed the following:

"It appeared from these experiments that the offspring did not tend to resemble their parents in size, but always to be more mediocre than they – to be smaller than the parents, if the parents were large; to be larger than the parents, if the parents were small."[44]

Francis Galton

This seems counterintuitive, but it is a classic case of regression to the mean. It is not about genetics, it's about statistics. Galton had expected to see offspring resembling their parents in size. Instead, he found that, with parents who were unusually tall, the offspring tended to be shorter than their mother and father. And with parents who were shorter than usual, many of the offspring were taller. A tall mother's height is partly caused by genetic factors, and partly due to random factors (and environmental influences) which made her grow taller than average during childhood. The genetic part of her height will pass to her child, but the random or environmental factors will not, making it more likely that her child will be shorter.

///////// RANDOMNESS IN EVERYTHING /////////

Pick up any business book in your favourite book store. Many of them (certainly not all) will try their best to convince you about the merits of some new management instrument.

Typically, the author selects real-life examples of companies that have seemingly outperformed the competition over time as proof for the efficacy of their brainchildren.

While there is certainly merit to some science on success factors, research often falls prey to regression to the mean. Take, for example, management thinkers who pick companies based on past performance and claim to have identified success factors for their past achievements. Jim Collins' bestselling book *Good to Great*[45] features eleven companies that have outperformed the rest over a period of time. Collins singles out five differentiators or success factors that he considers responsible for the difference of performance. What can we learn from analysing winners? Our common sense says: "A lot." But common sense can sometimes lead us astray.

Michael Cusumano, a professor at MIT's Sloan School of Management, uses a simple exercise to help students see the importance of accounting for both skill *and* luck as drivers for successful outcomes. On day one of his Advanced Strategic Management course, he typically asks his students to stand up. He then tells them he's going to toss a coin, and asks them to choose heads or tails.

He tosses the coin, reveals the side that came up, and asks the losers to sit down. After a number of rounds, there are usually only one or two students left standing. He then asks these winners to come to the front of the class and give an elaborate explanation on their success factors. By then, everyone clearly understands that the last students standing were merely lucky.

A team of three management thinkers, Raynor, Ahmed and Henderson took a closer look at the companies prominently highlighted as 'best-in-class' in popular management books such as *Good to Great, In Search of Excellence* or *What Really Works*. By looking at the total shareholder return (a measure for company performance), they confirmed that luck was an important, and mostly ignored, reason for company success.[46] The smaller the sample size (numbers of years with above-average success) and the bigger the role of luck relative to skill, the more difficult it is to determine best practices.

It is unsurprising, then, that many of Jim Collins' favoured companies from 2001 have since fallen from grace. One of his top picks was Fannie Mae, the giant mortgage lender that needed to be placed into conservatorship by the Federal Housing Finance Agency in the wake of the financial crisis. Another was Circuit City, which is now bankrupt.

//////////////////////// CHECKLIST //////////////////////////

Regression to the mean

 ## WHAT SHARE OF THE SUCCESS COULD BE DUE TO CHANCE?

Think about the process that leads to the outcome. What part of the outcome could have been the result of pure randomness? On the continuum of skill versus luck, where would you place the activity (stock picking, baseball, selecting your best-performing employee)? The location of the activity on the continuum will indicate the degree of mean reversion you need to expect.

 ## CAN YOU LOSE INTENTIONALLY?

One trick that Michael Mauboussin recommends in his book *The Success Equation* is to ask: "In this game, can I lose intentionally?"[47] Or even better: "What *proportion* of the time can I lose intentionally?" At poker, you can. At roulette, it's not possible. If you've found a situation in which you can lose intentionally, there's good news. The outcome of that situation is not *completely* due to chance. The more certain you are of your ability to lose intentionally, the more skill plays a role.

 ## DO YOU HAVE HISTORICAL DATA?

Do you have access to more data points, for example by looking at the past? The longer you can observe the process and its outcomes, the more confident you will be about which observation will count as an outlier. A solid foundation of historical data will help you set a baseline from which outliers are easier to spot.

WHAT'S THE COUNTERFACTUAL?

It is important to ask what could have happened but didn't. In the absence of intervention (implementation of the strategy or the policy), how would the metric, such as the stock price, the crime rate or the unemployment rate, have developed? It is typically easier to establish counterfactuals by analysing comparable companies, countries or individuals who have *not* received the intervention. In the absence of it, how did the outcome metric develop here?

FURTHER EXAMPLES

Scold and praise

Let's say you are coaching your talented daughter in gymnastics. For the next European Championships, she will need to practise performing her vault. After performing a beautiful handspring double front somersault tucked, you praise her on the assumption that praise will motivate her to do even better next time. But surprisingly, after a very good jump, she will usually do worse.

And the opposite is true, too. If you scold her after a particularly bad performance, she will most likely do better in the next round. It is tempting to conclude that your praise and scolding have resulted in a certain type of observable performance. But the difference in the gymnastic performance of your daughter can simply be attributed to regression to the mean.

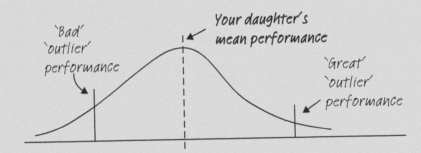

Your daughter's performance moves somewhere around her individual average performance. That's where most of the mass of the bell curve above lies. A really good performance is likely to be a positive outlier, just like a very bad performance. As such, after a very bad performance, it is likely that she will do better than before – and vice versa. This is generally not because of you scolding or praising, but simply due to a statistical fact.

Traffic safety

Imagine you are the president of a large city's transit authority. Accidents at one particular junction in the city have caused a particularly high number of traffic accidents over the last two years – some of them even fatal.

You call in your advisors to discuss options to bring down the number of accidents and make the junction safer. One of your advisors is able to convince you to put up speed cameras on two roads leading to the junction.

Sure enough, the accident rate starts to fall over the following months. So was it a good idea to install the speed cameras? It is tempting to assume so. After all, the fall in accidents occurred *after* the cameras had been put up.

But think about it again. Speed cameras are often installed as a *response* to an *exceptionally* high number of accidents in the periods before. But if there haven't been any other fundamental changes to the traffic flow, the increase in accidents is likely to be simply a statistical anomaly. In other words, we would expect the number of accidents to return back to base levels *anyway*. We would see the numbers of crashes regress to the mean. The upshot is that the speed cameras might have had an impact, but likely a much smaller one than we think.

The chart below makes it clear. By focusing on a certain junction with a high-accident rate, you are more likely to select an outlier. Say the long-term average number of crashes is around five to six, but it had a record number of nine accidents in 2013.

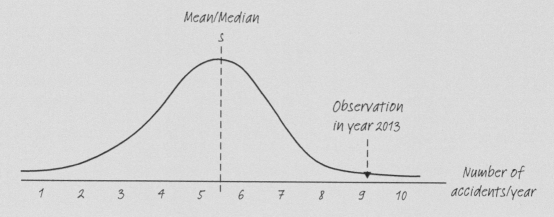

But because of its outlier nature, the number of accidents will naturally go down over the next year. It is important to note, though, that it is not *certain* that they will go down. It is just vastly more *likely* that they will go down to four, five, six or seven accidents in the next year.

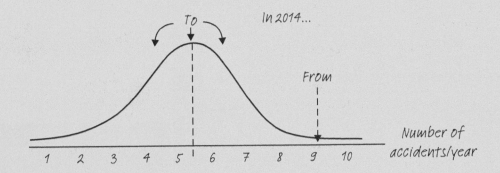

As the transit authority's president, how do you find out the true effect of installing speed cameras on traffic accidents? There are two ways. If you have sufficient data from the same site going back in time, you can establish a baseline and verify if the nine accidents per year are actually the norm or the exception. Or, you could compare the intersection with a control situation, i.e. another high-accident site where *no* additional speed camera has been set up. The key here is picking the right pairs for comparison to establish a true counterfactual.

THE BOTTOM LINE

We are programmed to automatically look for patterns in data. But we often impose patterns on what is, in fact, random. Establishing rules that work reliably is difficult, particularly if you only have a few observations to build on, and if luck plays its part as well. To overcome regression to the mean, think about how much the success you are observing could be due to chance, hone counterfactual reasoning (what could have happened but didn't), and try to find more historical data points.

Chapter Six

See the big picture

Practise systems thinking

Remember, always, that everything you know, and everything everyone knows, is only a model. Get your model out there where it can be viewed. Invite others to challenge your assumptions and add their own.

Donella H. Meadows

BENEFITS OF THIS MENTAL TACTIC

This mental tactic helps you spot, analyse and shape systems. It's applicable wherever systems are at play. It is useful in four general ways:

- It lets you understand the causal influences of a problem, especially if it appears sticky and hard to overcome.

- It allows you to identify feedback loops that either grow, balance, or even destroy a system.

- It helps you find the most effective leverage points at which to influence a system.

- It's a visual language that helps with thinking and communicating.

This mental tactic can help with planning a logistics chain and modelling the aggregated behaviour of suppliers. It can inform governments designing new traffic rules for highways or social policy changes. Or it can support entrepreneurs launching two-sided marketplaces, in which the attractiveness to one side of the market increases with the number of users on the other.

Systems thinking helps open the box and illuminate cause-and-effect relationships among a system's multiple parts. It allows us to map out the inner workings using pen and paper, or simulate their behaviour using modelling software. Systems thinking can be the key to understanding deeply ingrained patterns and dynamics and can be used to model how trends emerge, products spread and diseases transmit.

But systems thinking is not only a diagnostic tool: it also reveals possible points for intervening in a system. Use this mental tactic both to design new systems, detect faulty ones and learn ways to correct them.

PRACTISE SYSTEMS THINKING

Political parties, companies, non-profits, working groups and entire societies are systems – networks of agents, connected by links between them. A system is a network that is more than just a collection of its parts.

As with biological systems, it is hard to predict how complex human systems will behave. That's because systems comprise multiple elements that are interdependent. They are connected to one another and interact in complicated ways that produce their own patterns of behaviour over time. This has important implications for anyone seeking to address problematic systems behaviour. Here are some examples:

- Interest-rate manipulation doesn't, in itself, boost employment, stabilise prices and foster long-term growth. Rather, it interacts with the economic system. And that system includes many additional elements besides interest rates, such as consumption patterns, policy changes, international trade, environmental influences and rate of technological change.

- Oil-exporting countries are not solely responsible for oil-price hikes. That action alone isn't sufficient to trigger spikes in oil prices around the globe. Global oil price also depends on the policies and consumption behaviours of oil-importing nations.[48]

- Drug addiction doesn't stem only from the failings or poor decisions of individual addicts. Causes also include forces in the large social system, such as the wider availability of drugs and the conditions that raise demand for drugs, including poverty and over-prescription from doctors.

FEEDBACK LOOPS

Much of a system's peculiar behaviour is driven by what are called *feedback loops*. By understanding feedback loops, we can understand why some processes seem to spiral out of control, while others stabilise. Over the following pages, we will dig deeper into the nature of feedback loops and introduce a language to map and solve them effectively: causal loop diagrams. By understanding relationships in a systems-thinking way, we can identify better interventions to address problematic system behaviours.

The reinforcing feedback loop

Feedback loops are the cornerstone of thinking in systems. They are chains of cause and effect, in which the previous effect represents the next cause. Hence, they are closed loops, unlike open loops where the last effect doesn't feed back into the system. The following visual example shows the first of the two general types of loops: the reinforcing feedback loop.

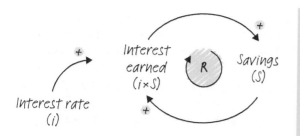

Reinforcing loops explain compounding interest: the higher the amount of savings in a bank account, the higher the interest earned, which in turn increases the total amount, earning even more interest. The results of exponential growth can often be astonishing: assuming a 5% interest rate, $100 grows to $13,150 in 100 years.[49]

Reinforcing feedback loops could also result in the opposite behaviour: rapid decline. Take, for example, the behaviour of the supervisor reacting to the performance of his employee. This feedback loop could go both ways. Praise and compliments could lead to enhanced motivation and increase in the performance, which again lead to positive reactions from the supervisor (and so on). But the opposite is also true: scold and chastisement could lead to further de-motivation of the employee, leading to a drop in performance.

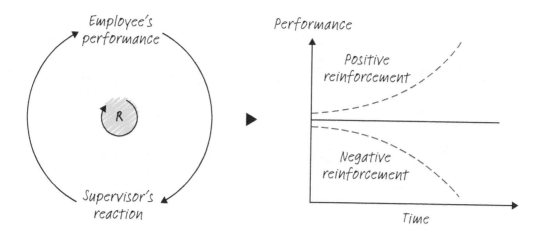

Feedback loops can also help explain the concept of a self-fulfilling prophecy, namely a forecast that causes itself to come true.

Let's take the situation above, but with two employees, A and B.[50] Both are on a similar path to promotion in a month and are similar in terms of seniority, ability and track record.

You are the manager and can only promote one. So you set out to use the upcoming month as a way to decide between both of them. A family emergency strikes A and requires him to work from home for the first week. It's an unavoidable consequence that you interact more frequently with B over the first week, implicitly providing more resources (attention, responsiveness, clues) to B than A. Given your busy time schedule, even after the return of A a week later, you subconsciously continue to provide more resources to B. After all, B has already done an outstanding job at the task you assigned her, you simply don't feel you need to invest in A.

After the end of the month-long trial period, you promote B, who has clearly done a better job. But was the competition actually fair, and was B the right person to promote? Looking at the system diagram, it becomes clear that the outcome is very sensitive to initial conditions. In this example, favour will quickly swing towards B. B will enjoy more resources and, as such, perform better at work, outstripping candidate A and the cycle begins again.

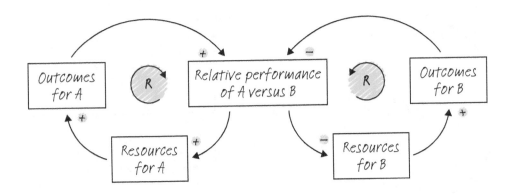

Balancing loops

The second kind of loop is known as a 'balancing loop'. As the term suggests, these are loops that bring the system to a desired target state – and keep it there.

A thermostat is the perfect example of a balancing (or goal-seeking) feedback loop.

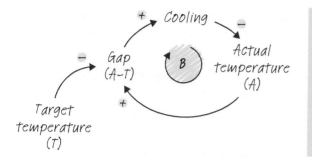

An air conditioning unit works by comparing the target with the actual temperature and cooling if a gap exists. Assume you start by setting the target temperature (T) to 72° F. The actual temperature (A) is 86° F, resulting in a gap A–T = 14° F. This will turn on the cooling mechanism, which in turn lowers the temperature and lessens the gap.

Let's take a look at an example that combines both types of loops – reinforcing and balancing – in the realm of workplace safety.

PUTTING IT INTO PRACTICE: WORKPLACE SAFETY[51]

John never thought this could happen to him. He had been with his employer, a large industrial construction company, for over 20 years, and inspection walks have always been part of his routine as a health and safety supervisor. As he was busy inspecting a site for a new factory in New Jersey, he tripped over a loose steel pipe that lay on the ground. John lost his balance and fell into the construction pit.

Luckily for him, he came out of the incident with just a few scratches. But as this was the third incident that year, John's accident alarmed the executive board who commissioned Marilyn, the head of on-site operations, to come up with a solution to systematically eradicate work-related injuries.

As a first step, Marilyn compiled statistics of work-related incidents across all the construction sites over the course of one year. Then she crunched the numbers in search for patterns. This allowed her to single out individual managers who were lax when it came to enforcing mandatory safety measures. But then she hit a wall: how should she go about finding the most important factors leading to workplace injuries and, more importantly, how could she eliminate them?

A friend pointed her to systems thinking, a methodology she was vaguely familiar with from her time at university. She was intrigued, as systems thinking promised to provide a more complete and effective way to understand and change the factors leading to accidents.

Marilyn went ahead and used a causal loop diagram (see image on the following page) to craft her strategy, analysing the many different factors affecting workplace safety levels and designing interventions to reduce the likelihood of accidents and injuries. Through interviews with site managers and the examination of work sites, she and her team discovered that, while managers were required to fill out reports after every accident, the reports lacked insights about what had *led* to that particular accident. Hence, the reports offered very few clues to determine ways to prevent each type of accident.

Marilyn knew that there had to be a better way to prevent accidents from happening. She examined the causal relationships and found three reinforcing feedback loops at work. Then, she actively looked for entry points that allowed her to intervene and shape the system.

Her analysis led her to propose incentives for employees that rewarded actively looking for, removing and reporting hazards encountered during their daily work. She also thought about penalties. Of course, cutting someone's paycheque is an unpopular endeavour. So Marilyn did the opposite, and created a construction site safety fund that would be paid out to the workers as an end-of-year bonus. Every type of safety incident (from actual accidents, to safety hazards like leaving tools or material on the floor) was assigned a cost that would be subtracted from the fund. Hence, workers would not only have an incentive to comply themselves, but also to hold others accountable.

Marilyn also discovered that many employees didn't take safety training all that seriously. She implemented a rigorous test for employees to take after their initial safety training, and involved senior management to communicate the new safety values.

Having employed the thinking systems mental tactic, Marilyn and her team managed to cut workplace-related accidents significantly.

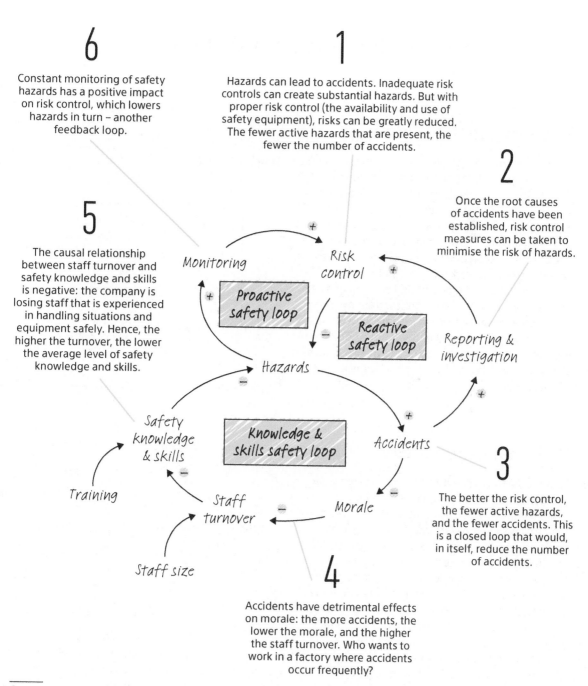

6

Constant monitoring of safety hazards has a positive impact on risk control, which lowers hazards in turn – another feedback loop.

1

Hazards can lead to accidents. Inadequate risk controls can create substantial hazards. But with proper risk control (the availability and use of safety equipment), risks can be greatly reduced. The fewer active hazards that are present, the fewer the number of accidents.

2

Once the root causes of accidents have been established, risk control measures can be taken to minimise the risk of hazards.

5

The causal relationship between staff turnover and safety knowledge and skills is negative: the company is losing staff that is experienced in handling situations and equipment safely. Hence, the higher the turnover, the lower the average level of safety knowledge and skills.

3

The better the risk control, the fewer active hazards, and the fewer accidents. This is a closed loop that would, in itself, reduce the number of accidents.

4

Accidents have detrimental effects on morale: the more accidents, the lower the morale, and the higher the staff turnover. Who wants to work in a factory where accidents occur frequently?

Source: Moizer, J.D. (1999) System Dynamics Modelling of Occupational Safety: A Case Study Approach

//////////////// FURTHER EXAMPLES ////////////////

The VHS–Betamax war

In the videotape format war, video cassette recorders (VCRs) competed ferociously for market dominance in the late 1970s and the 1980s. The major contestants were two fundamentally incompatible systems: VHS and Betamax. Eventually, VHS won and became the market standard. One advantage for VHS was the low price of their recorders, making them popular, causing strong network effects. People recorded TV shows and swapped tapes among each other. The more players of one type in your community, the bigger your incentive to buy the same type of player or recorder. VHS managed to cash in most of the net-work effects. The chart below shows the illustrative sigmoid curve (also called 's-curve') for the adoption of the two systems.

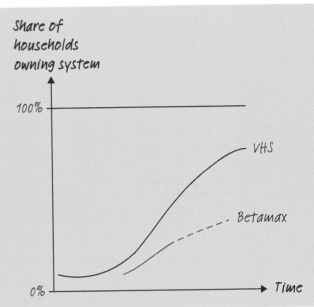

Personal productivity

Your productivity is measured by how much work you get done in an hour, a day or a week. It is simply output divided by input. Specific forces in the organisational system you're working in can affect your productivity. Let's say your boss wants you to deliver that project report by Wednesday, but you were under the impression that you had until Friday. In an effort to meet the strict deadline, you end up burning midnight oil over the next few days. Working overtime allows you to expedite your project and meet the deadline (a balancing loop), thus improving your productivity in terms of number of days required to complete the work (three days instead of five days). But it also leads

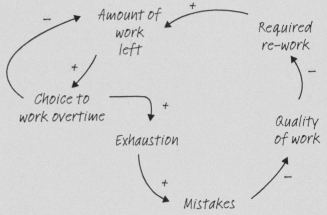

to fatigue, which can cause you to make mistakes that require rework. That could mean putting in even more overtime hours (a reinforcing loop).

SOLVING PROBLEMS USING THE SYSTEMS APPROACH

Let's use the following example to walk through a typical causal loop diagram. Take Sarita, an entrepreneur who developed a new exciting product, say, an electric skateboard. Sarita is trying to figure out how she can drive sales of her product.

1

What are you trying to explain?

Begin with a blank sheet of paper. What is the phenomenon you are trying to explain? In this case, Sarita aiming to build a model that helps explain customer growth. Start by writing down the goal metric in the centre of your sheet, in this case: # of customers.

2

Introduce variables

What are the most important factors that drive growth in Sarita's customer base? For now, just brainstorm the various factors that might play a role – awareness, quality of the product, price, etc. Note them down. The more direct the causation, the closer to the centre.

3

Establish causalities

How do the variables you identified in Step 2 interact with each other? For example, quality plays a role for product attractiveness, and so does price. Establish all the causalities you can think of and use arrows to visualise relationships.

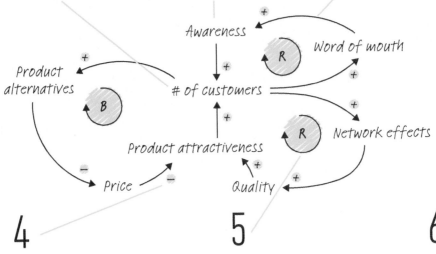

4

Set polarities

Now it is time to *qualify* the dependencies. If it is 'the more A, the greater B', the relationship is positive, if it is of the kind 'the more A, the lower B', it is a negative relationship. Higher quality (durability, battery time) increases product attractiveness, but a higher price decreases it. Indicate the polarities (+/-) by attaching a sign to the arrow.

5

Identify loops

Loops can either be reinforcing or balancing (goal-seeking). To identify a loop, start with one variable and follow the direction of the arrows. If you count an odd number of negative signs, you have encountered a balancing loop (B), if even, a reinforcing loop (R).

In our example, a larger number of users would most likely result in competitors with superior products, for example an electric skateboard with higher mileage entering the market.

6

Distil insights

Distil insights by analysing the interplay of feedback loops in your model. Is there an easy way Sarita can spur word of mouth publicity (a positive feedback loop), for example, by sending a free board to social media influencers who could help spread the word?

///////////////////// THE BOTTOM LINE /////////////////////

Systems are groups of interdependent actors or items forming an integrated whole.[52] The environment, social groups and companies are all examples of systems. When mapping out systems, one typically starts by identifying causal chains such as 'A leads to B leads to C'. Whenever C has an effect (directly or indirectly) on A, we call them feedback loops. Feedback loops result in emergent behaviour such as exponential growth (reinforcing feedback loops) or convergence (balancing feedback loops). Depending on your aim, you typically try to create, change or stop causal loops. The systems thinking mental tactic lets you analyse loops and find the most effective points of intervention.

Part 3

Craft the approach

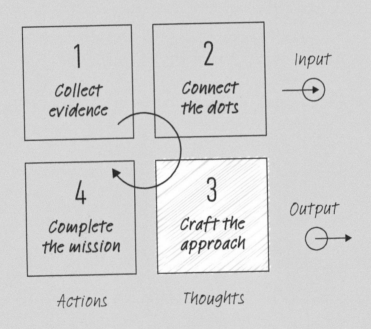

You have $100,000 – what's the best way to use it? Should you spend two years in your entry-level job or undertake postgraduate study? Should your company invest in a new machine or a new factory? How do you go about making the correct decision? How can you test possible solutions in the real world?

In the last two parts of the book, we've provided mental tactics that help you gather correct and relevant data as well as understand causal relationships. We are now at a critical juncture, the transition from *input* (collecting evidence and connecting the dots) to *output*. This part is all about making decisions, developing solutions and testing them in the real world.

In Chapter 7, we will start with a mental tactic fundamental to rational decision making: thinking on the margin. In Chapter Eight, we will introduce the scoring approach, a framework for making rational decisions. In Chapter Nine, we will look at experimentation as an agile way to test your solution in real life, before rolling it out on a large scale.

Our goal here is to help you take the information you've gathered and analysed in the previous two parts of the book and start to take action.

Chapter Seven

Think on the margin

Focus on the next unit

The judgement of value refers only to the supply with which the concrete act of choice is concerned.

Ludwig von Mises

BENEFITS OF THIS MENTAL TACTIC

Thinking on the margin is a fundamental tactic for rational decision making. It requires you to only take into account variables that are pertinent to your situation (rather than those that are set in the past and hence unchangeable). In its core, marginal thinking is economic thinking, as it always assumes that decisions are made by weighing *additional* costs against *additional* benefits. We often fall into the all or nothing trap in which we consider *all* the benefits and *all* the costs of a decision situation, which not only renders them very complex (and computationally heavy), but also leads to flawed decisions.

When *not* to use this mental tactic

There are some situations in which making decisions on the margin is not sensible. Consider the fashion retailer Nordstrom, renowned for its laissez-faire return policy. Nordstrom's customer satisfaction guarantee includes full reimbursement of returned products even without receipts, often years after the purchase. At the margin, Nordstrom shouldn't accept these refunds: the marginal costs of paying refunds for used clothes that might be unsaleable results in a marginal net loss. But taking into account the reputational benefit of the liberal return policy, Nordstrom's approach might lead to an increase in overall profits and greater customer satisfaction.

FOCUS ON THE NEXT UNIT

Suppose we offer you the choice between a glass of water and a bar of gold. What a question, you think. Of course, you'd choose gold over water. You have intuitively made a *marginal* decision. It's likely that for you gold carries a much higher market value than water. But what if you were asked this question during a multi-day trip through the Sahara desert without any liquids? The bar of gold would have no value for you in this situation as all you long for is water.

How do you think on the margin? Marginal in this context means additional. By thinking on the margin, you are considering the effect the next additional (or incremental) unit has on you. For an Uber driver, the cost of earning an extra hour's pay at the end of a long day is much higher than at the beginning of her their shift. They are tired and their back aches, which makes a *marginal* hour of driving at the end of their shift much more arduous.

It turns out that the price set for a product is, at least among neoclassical economists, exactly equal to its marginal utility. The marginal utility is the amount of satisfaction, pleasure or benefit people get out of consuming *the next unit* of it. So, it is not the fact that water in itself is abundant, but that the pleasure of consuming one unit of water for the typical person is lower than the pleasure that people take from a unit of gold. The reason being, most people are sufficiently hydrated *in the given moment* and, in most places, water is in ample supply. We can rely on our water systems working tomorrow just as they do today and we trust that supermarkets will continue to stock affordable bottles of water.

You may think: what's the value of this chapter when I already intuitively make decisions on the margin? What extra value can it bring? Well, it turns out that most of us are actually really bad at thinking on the margin. We often take the past too much into account, either to tell a consistent story to ourselves, or because the past appears to be intimately linked to future decisions.

THE BUILDING BLOCKS OF MARGINAL THINKING

Marginal units

Instead of considering the total or average amount in every decision, the marginal thinker is only concerned with the additional unit, such as the next hour of driving, the next piece of pizza, or the next investment. One of the fascinating characteristics of marginal units is that they are what economists describe as typically *decreasing in whatever input factor is required.*

What does that mean? For example, take eating pizza. The first slice will be delicious, and so will the second, third and fourth. Soon you'll be getting full, and the *next* (marginal) slice of pizza won't be as satisfying as the first one. In the chart below, the vertical distance, measuring satisfaction (or, as an economist would term it 'utility') declines with each extra piece of pizza – eventually even turning negative.

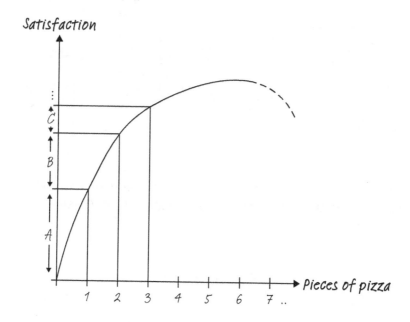

Or consider an energy company active in oil exploration. The first oil fields are easy to tap into as their location is known and their reservoirs are large and accessible (assume, to simplify, that all oil fields have oil reservoirs of equal sizes). Maximising their profits, the next (marginal) oil field project will be the ones that are *slightly* harder to access, and so on. At the end, the only fields that remain are those that are hardest to reach.

In the following chart are the expected exploitation costs and revenues for four oil fields. The lengths of the arrows indicate exploitation costs per site. The executive committee, acting on behalf of shareholders, would start with those projects promising highest profit first (oil field 1), and work their way downwards. The expected revenues of oil field 4 are below the exploitation costs, at least at the given moment. This may change as technology advances and then your marginal utility would change too.

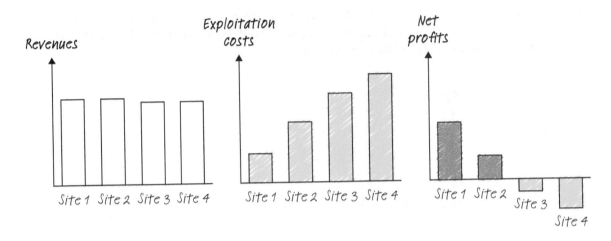

Marginal thinkers ask themselves: "What's the most value-adding activity I could spend my next five minutes on?", "How can I put this $100 to best use?" or "Given the current customer base, which customer should we take care of next?"

Sunk costs

Sunk costs are costs that have been incurred as a result of past decisions. They are unrecoverable. Because they happened in the past, they are different from the other costs a company faces, such as R&D or materials. They are independent from any event in the future. Sunk costs have been incurred no matter what you choose to do next. They cannot be influenced.

Even though we talk about costs here, what is meant is any kind of outlay (time or attention) expended to bring about a better result in the future. A cost could be learning a skill, for example. Say you are told that an attractive business position opened up in Latin America. The deal is sealed, and in a year from now, you and your family plan to move to Mexico City. In anticipation of your new role, you invest many hours per week in learning Spanish. However, due to bad luck, the position in Mexico City falls flat. At this junction, it is natural for most of us to say to ourselves, "Well, I've already invested at least 200 hours in learning Spanish. I might as well make the most out of it and continue to practise it. You never know!"

But it is actually not the most rational thing to do, unless you really enjoy learning languages or anticipate that knowing Spanish will be advantageous to your future career or life. The fact that you have learned Spanish in the past should not *in itself* be enough reason to continue to do so. Assuming you don't benefit in speaking Spanish in any other way, the costs of learning

Spanish are sunk and unrecoverable. You simply can't undo the past, or allocate the cost (your time spent practising) in any other way.

Humans tend to hold on too tightly to their past decisions and hence fall into the sunk cost fallacy. We do this because our mind subconsciously connects decisions that are related, even if they are in the past and don't make a difference for *future* decisions. Marginal thinkers are only interested in the *future* outcomes of their decisions and *future* trade-offs. They don't have any allegiance to whatever happened in the past.

How can you address this? Armed with *The Decision Maker's Playbook,* you can take on a new role in your organisation: the sunk cost bias police. Whenever you hear someone saying something like, "We've already spent so much time on this" or "We spent a lot of money setting up the business in Angola," you can be virtually certain that sunk cost bias is at work. We've found it helpful to respectfully but directly intervene at those moments by saying: "That's actually not the point. That time and money is gone. The question is whether the next dollar or hour we are about to invest is worth it, knowing what you know right now."

Decreasing marginal returns

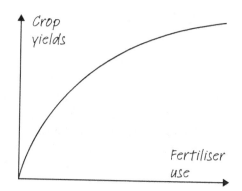

This idea is key to marginal thinking. In fact, without decreasing marginal returns there would not be the need to think at the margin.

Decreasing marginal returns are ubiquitous in life. For example, fertiliser improves crop production, but only up to a point. The more fertiliser you add, the lower the impact produced per unit of fertiliser and overkill can even reduce the yield.

The same is also true of the satisfaction we get from activities. Riding a rollercoaster is fun for a few minutes, maybe even an hour. After that time, it quickly gets less exciting.

Even the satisfaction of being on holiday, something most us look forward to more than anything else, doesn't linearly increase with the duration of the holiday. It is fun to forget which week day it is during the first two weeks, sit at the pool, drink margaritas and live and let live, but after a while even this gets dull and one wishes to go back home (and potentially even back to work).

The same is true for the satisfaction we derive from income. We often imagine that more money is better, and that we cannot have too much of it. One of the best-known studies on the relationship between happiness and income levels was done by Betsey Stevenson and Justin Wolfers in 2013. On a life satisfaction scale from 0 to 10, doubling your income doesn't translate into doubling your happiness. Rather, it buys you half a point on the scale. Stevenson and Wolfers illustrate this using an example: "GDP per capita in Burundi is about one-sixtieth that in the United States; hence a $100 rise in average income would have a twenty-fold larger impact on measured well-being in Burundi than in the United States."[53]

Marginal thinkers are very aware of the shifting trade-offs as time goes by (as they move up the line), and ready to make decisions on the margin – only taking into account their *current position*.

Opportunity costs

The concept of opportunity costs is closely related to marginal thinking. Let's say you have one hour available this afternoon to be productive. You could *either* tidy up your inbox and reply to emails *or* improve your Spanish. Note that as a function of time invested, both of these activities have *decreasing marginal returns* just like the yield/fertiliser mentioned. Typing away for a whole hour will make you tired. Holding constant the quality of your replies, the twentieth email will take longer than the first. And for your vocabulary skills, the bottleneck will be your brain's capacity to process and successfully memorise new terms.

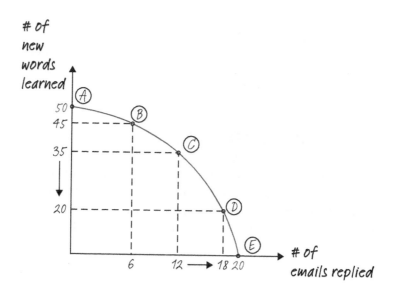

So, for both tasks, email replying and vocabulary memorising, the effectiveness will decline over time. This is exactly why the curve on the previous page is concave. Let's look at an example. Say you are at point B, which allows you to use the next hour to send 6 emails and learn 45 new words in this hour. And let's say your holiday to Costa Rica is coming up and you'd like to maximise the number of new words you learn. How many email replies do you have to *give up* in order to learn 50 words per hour? The cost of learning five more words is six emails. The easiest way to remind yourself about opportunity costs is to ask, "What am I giving up to get this thing? Is that a rational trade?"

Note that the opportunity costs differ based on your starting position. *On the margin,* if you are at point C, your opportunity costs for one additional word are just 6/10 emails, – half the price than if you were on point A. Marginal thinkers keep opportunity costs in mind (the benefits you would have received had you taken another course of action) to make best use of their time.

//////////////////// CHECKLIST //////////////////////

Marginal thinking

 ## CONSIDER YOUR CURRENT SITUATION

Making decisions on the margin requires you to consider your current situation. Note that it is not important how you got there, but simply where you are. What's the status of the presentation for your boss? How far along are you in the infrastructure project? Understanding one's situation and the cost and benefits of action *from where you are* is crucial for marginal thinking.

 ## LOOK FORWARD

It doesn't matter how much money or time you have already put into a project: you can't go back and change it. Time and money are considered sunk. You should only consider the *additional* benefit and compare it with the *additional* cost.

 ## MAP YOUR OPTIONS

Going forward, what are your options? Let's assume you could either put another hour into cleaning your house or start reading the book that's been lying on your desk for a few weeks. On the margin, reading the book might have a higher benefit to you, assuming your house is already pretty tidy.

 ## DON'T THINK IN BLACK AND WHITE

Life decisions are rarely black or white but usually somewhere in between. When deciding what to eat, you don't ponder between fasting and splurging, but whether to order that extra chocolate mousse after dinner or not.

FURTHER EXAMPLES

Hotel room prices

In the hotel business, operating at maximum capacity is the most important lever to generate revenues. A hotel cannot adjust the number of rooms (these are fixed costs), and the typical expenditures associated with an additional guest (check-in, cleaning, catering) are small compared to the extra revenues gained. Imagine that the extra costs per customer are $50, and the typical price per night is $200. Late at night and off-season, a traveller arrives with only $100 in his pocket. Should the hotel accept the offer? The answer is yes. On the margin, it is profitable for the hotel to do so, even though £100 is somewhat below the regular price per night.

Income taxes

Most governments earn income taxes using a progressive tax system. The tax rate on the additional dollar earned increases with income. For example, in the USA the 2019 tax rate for incomes from $0 to $9,700 was 10%, while the marginal tax rate on earnings over $510,300 was 37%. Using progressive tax systems, countries usually try to curb inequality, because higher-income households have to pay more taxes relative to their income than lower-income households. For freelancers and hourly-paid professionals deciding how many hours to work, it makes sense to think on the margin. They would take home roughly 90 cents per dollar income if the marginal dollar is in the lowest tax bracket, while only 63 cents in the highest tax bracket.

Buying a pair of shoes

Suppose you are looking for a pair of shoes to buy. You really like the ones priced $100 a pair. As you are about to go to the checkout, the shop assistant approaches you and makes you an offer: two pairs for only $150. Although the average price for the pair has now dropped to $75, you should think on the margin. How much pleasure do you actually derive from the second pair? The first pair is clearly worth $100 or more to you, otherwise you wouldn't have bought them. But is the second pair worth the marginal $50, even though you hadn't planned to buy them in the first place?

THE BOTTOM LINE

When we make decisions, we often take into account irrelevant factors such as costs incurred in the past. We often fall into the all or nothing trap in which we consider *all* the benefits and *all* the costs of a decision situation, which makes decision problems complex and unwieldy. Contrast that with marginal thinking. It requires you to only take into account variables pertinent to your *current* situation. In its core, marginal thinking is economic thinking, as it always assumes that decisions are made by weighing *additional* costs against *additional* benefits. Marginal thinking provides the foundation for rational decision making.

Chapter Eight

Score points

Articulate your criteria and make sound trade-offs

I have been struck again and again by how important measurement is to improving the human condition.

Bill Gates

BENEFITS OF THIS MENTAL TACTIC

Making the right decisions between several options is never easy. But good decision making starts even further upstream – with the generation of valid alternatives. Here we introduce techniques to come up with options to choose from, go through the various types of criteria, and offer several scoring and ranking methods to make sound decisions.

ARTICULATE YOUR CRITERIA AND MAKE SOUND TRADE-OFFS

Building the USA's waterways one analysis at a time

In the 1930s, the US Army Corps of Engineers refined a new decision-making methodology to determine whether and when to take action – with effectively no input from the economics profession.

As is often the case, (legislative) necessity was the mother of invention. The Flood Control Act of 1936 required the Army Corps of Engineers to carry out certain projects for the improvement of the waterways when the benefits of the project exceeded the costs of the project. Pretty straightforward so far. Does the money heading out of the door lead to more money coming in the door? So the Corps were now obliged to figure out whether the farmers on the riverbanks, the citizens in neighbouring towns, the local county authorities and the businesses downstream were affected by a project, and to what extent.

Suddenly, the Corps needed a robust, repeatable method for understanding who benefitted – and how – from their proposed projects and who paid a price. This imperative led them to develop the approach we know today as cost–benefit analysis. Here we're going to introduce our favourite tools for making good decisions consistently, and learning from the decisions you've already made. Our goal here is to give you some process that, if practised consistently, will make you and your teams reliably better decision makers over time.

This represents an important transition in the book – from systematically amassing information and thinking about it clearly, to the process of *doing* and deciding. We present our approach to choosing between the many options that will present themselves. We want to introduce you to an approach that will help you to develop criteria to assess your options and then quantify the different trade-offs.[54]

GENERATE ALTERNATIVES

If you've read this far, you already know how to look for data and make sense of it. Now it's time to start thinking about solutions. To start with, generate alternatives – lots of them, even preposterous ones. In other words, we recommend you to go broad first, before converging, and carve out the possible set of solutions (or alternatives). There's good evidence that forcing your brain to generate multiple alternatives leads to better solutions in the longer term.[55] Ideas that pop into mind easily aren't necessarily the best ones (take a look at Chapter 2 on why having an idea that's too accessible might unduly limit you).

The simplest way to do this is a list, with no judgements, of every even remotely plausible idea that you can think of. If you're thinking about your career, options might look like this:

- Stay in my current job.
- Seek a promotion or different job at the same company.
- Find a job at a different company.
- Set up my own business.
- Generate enough successful investments to retire early.
- And so on ...

As soon as you do this, you will see that there are alternatives upon alternatives. There are myriad businesses you could set up, and endless companies other than your current one you could join.

If you choose to conduct this brainstorming exercise in a group setting (which we generally advise as this approach allows you to crowdsource options), ensure that you separate ideation from evaluation. What has worked best for us is handing out sticky notes to the participants, and starting with five to ten minutes of silent brainstorming, after which all ideas will be collected and clarified. Only then should a discussion and evaluation take place. This is to avoid 'group think', a common phenomenon that leads to an early (and undesirable) convergence of opinions.

Be clear about what you want, and how much you want it

Being clear about your objective really matters. Equally important is a clear approach to measuring and assessing this objective. We start from the assumption that everything *can* be measured.[56] Even in situations where measurement is extremely challenging, the rigour of assigning quantitative values or scores to your various options is incredibly helpful in the assessment process.

Some of the biggest failures in decision making and planning that we have seen over the years have arisen because of a failure to set strict criteria up-front. This includes failing to be clear about the type of criteria you are using. Let's illustrate the development of criteria with an example close to home – Simon's contemplation about what kind of car to buy. Note that here Simon has decided already to buy a car, he just wants to make the best choice.

Here is where a scoring model starts to come into play. Your definition of best is almost certainly different from Simon's definition. Simon starts out by defining his criteria, and listing questions to test this criteria. There are two types of criteria:

1 **Binary criteria:** in business, you might hear these referred to as must-haves or non-negotiables. In practice, you can think of these as yes/no questions that must be answered. They equally apply to personal choices (buying a car). In this instance, Simon has identified 'car must have airbags' as one of his criteria. The question is a simple one: does the car have airbags? If we were to show this criterion graphically, it would look like this.

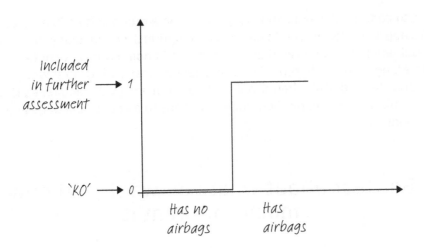

This type of criterion is very straightforward – the thing you want (or don't want) is either present or it's not. If it's not present, the option is knocked out (KO) and will not be considered any further.

A slightly more complex variant of this is the threshold criterion. It is different from the above, in that you only care about this criterion being above a certain point. If it's above this point (or below it, depending on how you frame it), it's KO and will not be included in any further consideration. For example, this could be a budget constraint or a minimum fuel consumption. As long as the car meets the threshold, he will consider it for further analysis. If not, it will drop out.

2 **Strictly improving or dis-improving criteria:** you can think of these as more is better or less is better criteria. A great example of a more is better criterion for Simon would be something like fuel economy: the more fuel-efficient the car is, the better.

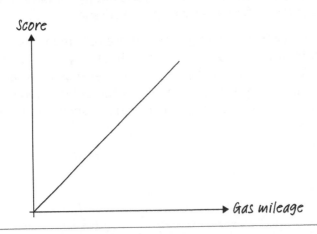

Now that you have your criteria and you are clear about what you want, it's time to start comparing them to one another and winnowing your list. Here is where scoring models come in. At its simplest, a scoring model is a way of assigning value to your various criteria, and using it to assess how your options compare. Here's how to build a scoring model.

1 **Generate a shortlist by using your binary criteria (filters):** your binary criteria, including threshold criteria, help you sweep options off the table. For example, you can now cross out all the cars on your list that do not have airbags (say a sad farewell to a 1960s Mustang convertible) or any cars not meeting the budget threshold (another sad farewell to that Aston Martin). This should help you whittle down your list.

2 **Define your weights and assign scores:** now that you know what you care about, you need to figure out how much you care. You can start by weighting your various criteria in one of the following ways:

- Assign a percentage value to each of the criteria.

- If you are doing this in a group, you can give everyone 10 points and ask people to allocate those points among the various criteria. This is particularly helpful to account for depth of sentiment. Perhaps Simon's partner feels that each of the criteria of airbags, fuel efficiency and price are equally important, whereas Simon only really cares about price.[57] In order to find the relative weight in percentage, you then need to divide the number of points per option by the total numbers provided to people.

- You can also select the two dimensions that matter most to you, and score each of your alternatives from 1 to 100.

3 **Plot your outcomes:** now that you have a weighting and a score for each of your criteria, you want to be able to visualise them, for example by using a 2x2 matrix. The purpose of this framework is to allow you to visualise comparisons between your various options in two dimensions and to understand where the trade-offs lie.

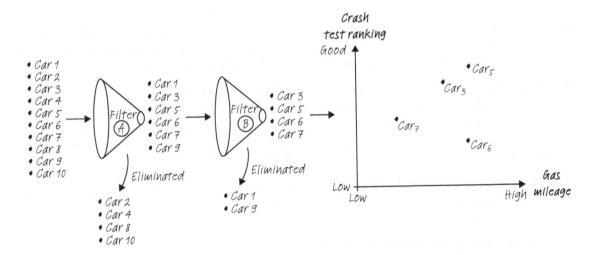

Since you've already knocked out the options that didn't make the cut (filter A and filter B in the visualisation above), you are only left with options that fare differently on the more-is-better dimensions. You could plot, as the example shows, the fuel consumption on the x-axis and the crash test ranking on the y-axis.

4 **Make your selection:** using the above matrix or one like it, you'll be able to readily see and discuss your choices. Some choices will be very clear – options in the bottom left of your matrix will almost always make sense to eliminate. Options in the top right will almost always be a winning strategy, and those should be the ones you look to pursue. At this point, you might be thinking that once you've created the matrix your choices will be obvious. We hope so, yes. The act of creating a matrix like the one above should high-light choices that are clear 'yesses' and clear 'nos.' But it should also generate those that warrant further discussion and require more nuanced trade-offs, such as car 3 and car 5, which are both in the top-right corner.

You might be thinking this matrix is terrific when you have two dimensions that you really care about, but what about the instance in which you have more (perhaps many more). This is common in evaluation decisions like choosing between candidates for a position, or understanding how the performance rating of one of your team members has changed over time. In that instance, we argue for the spider chart – a chart where multiple dimensions are used to increase or decrease the total area of the chart. Let's use the job candidate example. You might have multiple criteria, including:

- years of previous experience

- interpersonal skills

- presentation and communication skills

- technical understanding of the subject matter required for the role

- ability to work in fast-paced environments.

It's obvious that such a slate of criteria doesn't lend itself well to a 2x2 matrix. Instead, it is relatively straightforward to display it graphically in a spider chart. Here's what it looks like with one candidate's rating plotted – the further away you get from the centre of the graph, the better.

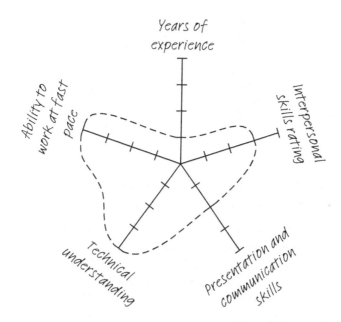

The next spider chart shows what it looks like with another candidate plotted too. Now you can start to see that having the most surface area (the biggest spider web) is generally more desirable. This general principle could change if your criteria were differently weighted. For example, you can see that our first candidate clearly beats our second candidate on surface area and thus seems to be the strongest candidate. This would only change if for some reason we had weighted years of experience far more heavily than other criteria.

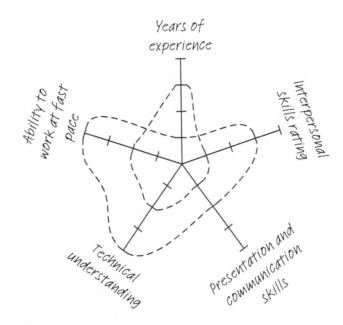

Spider charts are particularly useful when you have multiple options and multiple criteria and want to be able to visualise them simultaneously.

5 **Refine your criteria over time:** if you stick rigorously to this approach, you'll learn a lot about your criteria over time. For instance, criteria that you thought were very important initially might not matter at all (a project is so profitable that the difficulty to implement it will always be worth it). It might be that what you originally thought was an independent criterion (presentation and communication skills) is actually just a component of a different criterion (in this case, interpersonal skills). Over many rounds of the same decision, you'll start to notice which criteria are truly sensitive. You might expand or eliminate criteria based on this reflection.

USING FORCED RANKING TO MAKE SPEEDY CHOICES TOGETHER

For low-stakes decision situations, use *forced ranking*. Forced ranking is particularly suitable for situations where you are trying to identify a compromise outcome between multiple parties whose interests might not be the same. Conventional scoring models, where you pre-agree the weightings (or interests) up-front do not have this feature built in. In the process of writing this book, we often had to break for lunch. And, because we prefer to continue our discussion over lunch, we wanted to eat together. But our preferences are not the same, and our criteria for a good lunch spot are not the same. For example, if we were to go through the above, detailed exercise, Simon's criteria might include:

- vegetarian-friendly
- calorie-dense
- within 10 minutes' walk of our current location.

Julia's might include:

- omnivore friendly
- very spicy
- not messy.

It isn't necessarily helpful to create a scoring model for these criteria, and to search around comprehensively for a suitable restaurant. Instead, you can use forced ranking:

1 Jointly generate a selected number of alternatives (three to five seems about right here).

2 Ask each participant to rank the options, from 1 to n (up to however many options you have).

3 Add the ranks assigned to each option together – the option with the lowest score (most preferred) wins.

Note that in a forced ranking model, we don't really care *why* each person selected the rankings that they did, our goal is just to quickly find out what people prefer so we can take action.

OPTION	SIMON	JULIA	
Mexican	1	2	← winning choice
Chinese	3	1	
Italian	2	4	
Korean	4	3	

Our approach of forced ranking and then a head-to-head comparison of the options ensures that you choose the option that optimises everyone's preferences. In this case, Mexican food is what is called a *pareto-optimal* solution, where no one can be made better off without making someone else worse off.

The forced ranking approach assumes that each decision maker's preferences count equally. But what if that isn't the case? You can also consider supplementing the forced ranking approach with a veto right. For example, let's say that we have decided that Simon's preference for a vegetarian restaurant outweighs other criteria and Julia's preferences, so you might give Simon the right to veto a restaurant selection from the list (a steakhouse), even before a forced ranking is conducted.

But what about a situation where someone's preferences might actually count *less* than someone else's? Let's stick with lunch for a moment. Simon isn't really interested in weighting criteria, scouring Google Maps for a comprehensive set of options and prowling TripAdvisor to prioritise among the various choices. So, instead, he asks Julia to read *her* list of preferences aloud and shouts out 'stop' when she comes to a choice he is ok with. We'll never know if this was the optimal solution for Simon – there could have been something he would have preferred further down Julia's list, but it is a good enough solution. It might look like Julia's preferences will always trump Simon's preferences here. You might ask if that is fair to Simon. In fact, Simon's preferences are being taken into account – it is just that we are weighting his preference not to spend his time, attention and energy on deciding where to eat. He cares about this more than where we actually eat.

The above example is a simple one (but a very frequent decision that people find difficult to make), but you can also use it for major decisions. Consider, for example, selecting the location of a new building for your office – an important financial decision, but also an emotional one. Having each member of your team conduct a forced ranking independently will inevitably spark a conversation about the different trade-offs each person is making, and why. Encouraging decision makers to reveal their preferences by placing various options in relation to one another can be instantly clarifying, and can force a conversation about what is important to each party, and why.

WINNERS AND LOSERS: COST-BENEFIT ANALYSIS

Let's return to our Army Engineers, busy building bridges and dams all over the USA. Recall the legislative requirement that if a project benefits *to whomsoever they accrue* exceed the costs, it should be undertaken. Suddenly our Army Engineers aren't asking themselves if a project is beneficial for the Army, or even good for the US Government; they are instead conducting a comprehensive accounting of who benefits, in what way and how much.

While this approach might seem sensible for a government entity, who should theoretically be trying to maximise the general welfare, some of you will be questioning the wisdom of this approach for private organisations. What good is it if a project's total benefits outweigh the total costs if your organisation bears all the costs and someone else (customers, competitors) receives all the benefit? Well, the advantage comes in your ability to charge your customers and competitors for this benefit. You have determined that the project creates more benefits than costs. The next step is to determine how to ensure that you can recoup some of those costs from the people or groups who have benefitted.

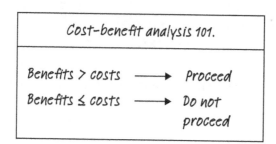

We didn't set out to write a project finance textbook (and we don't think you set out to read one) but bear with us for a little maths here. You are trying to decide if your company should buy a new machine that mixes and bakes both Pfeffernüsse (a cookie from Simon's native Germany) and Lamingtons (a cake from Julia's native Australia). The machine costs $10,000 to buy and you will need to pay your baker $1,000 per week. You can produce 600 Pfeffernüsse and 700 Lamingtons per month. This is a case where the benefits can be monetised – you can sell them both for $1 each. If you embark upon this project, you'll be committed to it for at least 10 years. You're sinking your life savings into this machine: do the benefits outweigh the costs?

1 First, quickly capture your benefits and costs, in the same way we have on the previous page.

2 Second, we want to be able to compare benefits in year 10 with costs that we incur today. We do this by identifying the present value of our benefits and costs. Stay with us for the quick maths tutorial:

- Discount your benefits and costs based on the time value of money. We operate on the principle that a pound today is worth more than a pound in a year's time. The reason? We all prefer money sooner over money later. And if you invest that money at a risk-free yearly real interest rate r, you will receive your money times (1+r) in a year's time. Hence, money paid in one year is worth *today* that amount *divided* by (1+r).

- For simplicity, we are going to set the discount rate at 10% per annum using the following formula.

$$Net\ present\ value\ (NPV) = (Value\ of\ benefit - costs)/(1+r)^t$$
$$where\ r = discount\ rate\ (e.g.\ 10\%)$$
$$and\ t = relevant\ time\ periods\ (e.g.\ \#\ of\ years)$$

Still confused? Don't worry, cost–benefit analysis is a little counterintuitive at first. Here it is as a table.[58]

DESCRIPTION	YEAR 0	YEAR 1	YEAR 2	YEAR 3	YEAR 4	YEAR 5	YEAR 6	YEAR 7	YEAR 8	YEAR 9	YEAR 10	TOTAL
Costs-new machine $10,000	$10,000											$10,000
Costs-baker's salary ($1,000 per month ($12,000 per year)	-	$10,909	$9,917	$9,016	$8,196	$7,451	$6,774	$6,158	$5,598	$5,089	$4,627	$73,735
Benefits-Pfeffernüsse sales $600 per month ($7,200 per year)	-	$6,545	$5,950	$5,409	$4,918	$4,471	$4,064	$3,695	$3,359	$3,054	$2,776	$44,241
Benefits-Lamington sales $700 per month ($8,400 per year)	-	$7,636	$6,942	$6,311	$5,737	$5,216	$4,742	$4,311	$3,919	$3,562	$3,239	$51,614

Now, subtract your total costs ($83,735) from your total benefits ($95,855). That simple calculation gives you a total net benefit of $12,120. The verdict? While this new baking machine might not be your ticket to untold riches, the costs do outweigh the benefits on a net present value basis. This quick maths took us no more than a few minutes and lets us immediately assess a decade's worth of potential investments and revenues.

///// MAKING CRITERIA WORK FOR YOU /////

- **Don't be a hostage to the outcome:** if you make changes to the criteria because you don't like the outcome, be transparent and overt about it.

- **Be sensitive:** clarify at the beginning which criteria really matter, and those that don't move the needle. For example, in the search for a new house, you might start out by thinking that you really need a sunny back garden. Upon analysis, you note that you only sat outside 3 days last year, and didn't really miss it the other 362 days. You also know that you would never pick a house with a sunny back garden in an undesirable neighbourhood if you could have a house without one in a desirable neighbourhood. Your decision is, in fact, not particularly sensitive to your weak interest in having a sunny back garden.

- **Manage complexity:** three criteria are better than seven. As above, focus on those that really matter.

CHECKLIST

How to figure out what matters

 SET CRITERIA

List what really matters to you. What will cause you to change your mind? The fewer criteria, the better.

 DECIDE WHAT TYPE OF CRITERIA YOU ARE WORKING WITH

Binary and threshold (as filters) or strictly improving?

 DO A FIRST SCREEN

Use your binary criteria to eliminate some of the options before going on to evaluate them on the other criteria.

 NOT ALL CRITERIA ARE CREATED EQUAL

Assign weights to criteria to reflect their relative importance for your decision.

 AVOID GROUP THINK

In decision situations where more than one participant is involved, ask your team to develop their assessments independently.

 USE FORCED RANKING

Do this as a way to elicit preferences and make quick decisions.

//////////////// THE BOTTOM LINE ////////////////

Many choices are not as straightforward as they seem at first. Equally, many decisions that appear complex or stressful can be radically simplified. Every option has a different set of advantages and disadvantages and often it's hard to pick the right one. A structured scoring model allows you to deliberately reflect on criteria, weights and scores, and provides you with a rigorous assessment approach. Using scoring models makes it easy to communicate and discuss choices and allows you to reach the most beneficial solution.

Chapter Nine

Walk the talk

Run experiments to test your solutions in the real world

Do not be too timid and squeamish about your actions. All life is an experiment. The more experiments you make the better. What if they are a little coarse and you may get your coat soiled or torn? What if you do fail, and get fairly rolled in the dirt once or twice? Up again, you shall never be so afraid of a tumble.

Journals of Ralph Waldo Emerson, 11 November 1842

BENEFITS OF THIS MENTAL TACTIC

Conventional wisdom is often misguided, and so-called best practices can lead to disappointment when conditions change. To ensure the solutions you crafted actually result in the outcomes you intend, you will need a smart way to test them. Experimenting allows you to do so quickly and economically, learn from the outcomes of the experiment, and adjust your approach as you roll out the solution.

At first glance, this mental tactic seems to belong in an earlier part of the book. But we believe you'll get the most out of it just before the implementation phases of projects. View experiments and pilots as segues from solution to implementation, as a feeling of one's way and of learning by doing.

Look at it this way: what's the worst that can happen? Even if an experiment fails, it's likely to produce valuable data that can be used to refine the next iteration of your solution.

Experiments replace guesswork, intuition and best practices with knowledge. Experimentation is at the heart of what software developers call agile development. Rather than planning all activities up-front and then sequentially, agile development emphasises running many experiments and learning from them.

Applying this mental tactic has a number of benefits:

1

It allows you to focus on actual outcomes
A successful project is not deemed successful because it is delivered according to a plan, but because it stood the test of reality.

2

It decreases re-work
Because the feedback cycles are short, potential errors or problems are spotted quickly and can be smoothed out faster than conventional project planning.

3

It reduces risks
Because of increased transparency throughout the implementation process, risks can be better managed than in a conventional project.

Running experiments is a time-consuming and often expensive endeavour. Only very specific situations lend themselves to experimentation.

RUN EXPERIMENTS TO TEST YOUR SOLUTIONS IN THE REAL WORLD

Constantin is the third-generation owner and director of a niche marketing and market research company for the beverage industry. Clients hire him to assess and develop branding strategies for bottled and poured drinks. His mission: creating the desire that makes thirsty customers choose his clients' bottles over others.

But what's the best way to do so? What's the right story to tell? What's the most convincing concept? The answers to these questions have changed over time.

His grandfather's trade, he recalls, was mostly an art: "Grandpa chose the design based on what he *thought* customers would prefer. He had good taste, and was clearly blessed with an eye for aesthetics. Back then, few people compared the sales figures before and after a design change. Our customers were happy when their product stood out. The market wasn't crowded, so any brand that was able to maintain a consistent, professional look and feel was likely to get a large share of the pie."

One generation later, as the company grew and competitors multiplied, pure reliance on intuition was no longer sufficient to be successful in the marketplace. Instead, according to his father, one needed to combine intuition *and* science. Constantin reflects, "Dad still relied on his natural intuition to suggest designs that resonated with the customers – maybe that runs in the family. But he was also an avid student of psychology and decision sciences. He adjusted imagery, colours and text to what researchers said was effective."

Contrast that with Constantin's work today: "Today, we have the tools to experiment and optimise a product down to the last detail. There are so many things that could make a difference: design, text, colour, material. I don't try to guess what could work. Instead, I'm simply putting a few thousand bottles out in various retail locations and collecting data to see what resonates most."

Constantin runs business experiments. First, he creates a few variants of the final design, such as five different labels. Then, he asks several supermarkets to place his bottle on the shelf (he tries to ensure that the types of customers frequenting the supermarkets are some-what comparable). Finally, he uses the data he receives back to determine which design works best. This insight allows Constantin to start full-scale production of the design that has already proven to be highly effective in his experiment. Experimentation and testing can be an incredibly valuable tool in the arsenal of any decision maker.

Decision situations that are of substantial impact, but to a certain degree reversible, are the perfect ground for experiments. This is particularly true if the environment you find yourself in is complex or changing. The basic idea behind experimentation, *trial and error* is only feasible if the costs of error aren't prohibitively high. If your potential choice is both important and hard to undo, take time to decide. We have already talked specifically about these types of situations and the suggested mental tactic: scoring methods.

TWO TYPES OF EXPERIMENTATION

Generally, there are two ways to test out your ideas through experimentation:

1 Running a randomised control trial (RCT), which measures the impact of changes (the treatment) by comparing the reaction of one group (the treatment group) with a group that is left untouched (the control group). You might have heard of A/B testing, which is web development jargon for a type of RCT, and is used to optimise web content.

2 Experimenting sequentially with the same group (or subject), changing parameters in different cycles and measuring its effectiveness.

RCTs are considered the gold standard for scientific inquiry, but they are unsuitable for most situations. As a starter, to ensure the results are actually useful, you need two sufficiently large groups to which subjects are being assigned in a fully randomised fashion. If you can't ensure full randomisation, it's still possible to experiment, but you will need to pay attention to the distortions caused (for example, by self-selection of one type of participant into either the treatment or control group).

Sequential experimentation is easier and more pragmatic, but the results are less reliable and the experiments take longer to run. During RCTs, the treatment is compared with the non-treatment *at the same time,* whereas sequential experimentation is compared, well, sequentially. As such, the context factors might have changed in the second run. But for some interventions, sequential experiments are simply the only way to test their efficacy.

Let's take a look each of these approaches.

Finding optimal price points using randomised control trials

Professor Stefan Thomke and Jim Manzi, some of the most vocal advocates of experimentation in business settings today, describe PetCo's innovation culture in their 2014 *Harvard Business Review article.*[59]

Executives at Petco, a large pet food chain, are known for running over 75 business experiments per year. Each person responsible for running an experiment is asked to list the ways that their experiment, if successful, would contribute to the company's mission of being more innovative.

For every experiment, Petco selects 30 stores at random (the treatment group) and then matches 30 similar stores based on their size, customer demographics, regional competitors and so on (the control group). Then, Petco conducts blind tests, i.e. tests that are not even revealed to the managers and staff of the respective stores. Blind studies, which are standard in the medical industry, lower the (undesired) tendency of study subjects to modify their behaviour in experimentation settings.

This experiment set-up allows Petco to examine and optimise everything from price modifications to store layouts, opening hours and special offers. In one experiment, Petco found out that – everything else being equal – goods with prices that ended in 25 cents were highest grossing. The result went sharply against the grain of the conventional wisdom that prices should end in 99 cents or 95 cents. Senior leaders were sceptical of that result at first, but were willing to give the new pricing scheme a try. The result: after the roll-out had been executed (beginning with stores that were similar to the treatment group), sales for these products jumped by more than 24% after six months. You don't know what you don't know – until you test it!

CHECKLIST

How to run a randomised control trial (RCT)

 ## STATE THE HYPOTHESIS OF YOUR STUDY

What is it you are trying to find out? It is important to formulate your specific hypothesis before the start of the study. For example, your hypothesis might be that the modest increase in price (+10%) will *not* have a significant negative effect on your sales.

 ## DEFINE YOUR OUTCOME VARIABLE

Experiments allow you to establish a link between the change of an input factor (such as the price) on an outcome metric (such as the sales). In plain English: they help us understand what causal effect our actions have.

Typical outcome variables are unit sales or revenues, click-through rates (if you are optimising websites), number of people cared for (in terms of housing, healthcare), self-reported quality of life, customer satisfaction and so on.

CREATE TWO GROUPS: TREATMENT AND CONTROL

To measure what effect a treatment has, you need two groups that share similar traits: one treatment group (receiving the intervention or treatment) and one control group (receiving no intervention, or only a placebo).

It is important that both groups are selected *randomly*. Ideally, membership of any subject is determined completely by chance. This is easier said than done. In many cases *self-selection* takes place, in that individuals sharing certain traits are more likely to be part of either the treatment or the control group. This skews the results, because certain shared peculiarities of the subject groups (such as socio-cultural factors, place of residence, or simply availability at time of experiment) can be the sole explainers for the difference between groups, rather than the treatment.

In order to achieve statistically significant results, you need a sample size that is large enough. There are complicated formulas to calculate the optimal sample size, but as a rule of thumb, 30 to 50 observations is typically deemed sufficient in business contexts.

 ## ADMINISTER THE TREATMENT TO ONE GROUP

After randomly assigning your subjects to either treatment or control group, it is time to adjust the input of the treatment group, while leaving the input of the control group unchanged. In our example, you would increase the prices of a given product (or product category) by 10% in 20 random stores around the country.

Make sure you select a timeframe that is suitable to measure effects. A day would be too short, a year perhaps too long.

 ## MEASURE AND COMPARE

After the pre-defined time period has passed, gather the output data (in our example, sales) and calculate the averages. If the assignment of samples to treatment and control group was indeed fully random, then the treatment effect (for a 10% price increase) is simply the difference between the average outcomes of the treatment group and the average outcomes of the control group.

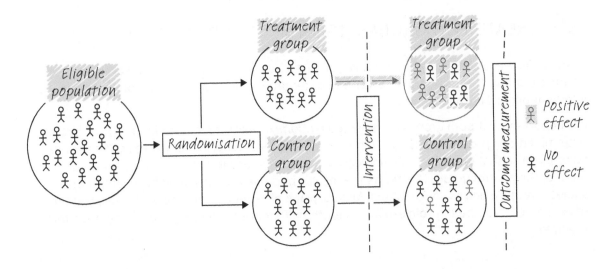

MEASURING THE IMPACT OF EATING HABITS ON SLEEP

Let's take a closer look at the second type of experimentation, sequential testing, by taking sleep quality as an example.

It shouldn't come as a surprise that recent research confirms the importance of sound sleep on cognitive functions and general wellbeing. Let's say that you are interested in optimising your sleep quality. There are a number of different ways of going about it.

Common sense/ intuition	Casual theories	Scientific tests	Real-life experiments
Vague sense or feeling about what is effective	Casual model, based on logic	Scientific study in different environment	Experiment with context comparable to actual application

Trusting your intuition and common sense is a first step. Here are some common-sense ideas: darken your bedroom, eliminate night-time noise and avoid eating large quantities of food just before bedtime.

The next level of sophistication is causal theories that appear to inherently make sense. It is plausible, for example, to assume that every human is equipped with a self-regulating sleep cycle. Under that assumption, if you find yourself repeatedly sleeping in when not using an alarm clock, you might reasonably conclude that your body naturally desires a longer sleep period. Allowing yourself to go to bed early (or wake up late) could also increase your sleep quality.

The next level could be to consult the scientific literature. By looking at textbooks and studies, you will quickly learn about circadian rhythms and REM sleep phases, and potentially identify ways to further optimise your sleep.

But because human bodies typically differ in important ways from the statistical average, there's real value in trying things out for yourself. For example, you could experiment with all those methods listed above. Or try out other interventions such as changing the foods you consume (carbohydrates versus proteins) prior to bedtime, varying the room temperature or using over-the-counter drugs such as melatonin.[60]

//////////////////// CHECKLIST ////////////////////

How to run n=1 experiments[61]

 ### START WITH DEFINING A RESEARCH HYPOTHESIS

What is it you would like to find out? Let's say you are currently completing your executive MBA at a renowned university, and are interested in boosting your cognitive faculties. One way to do so, so you have read, is by practising meditation on a regular basis. But based on your unrepresentative survey among friends (and internet forums), it doesn't seem to work for everyone.

 ### THINK ABOUT HOW TO OPERATIONALISE YOUR EXPERIMENT

How are you going to measure your outcome variable? Measurements need to be:

a. **valid** – the degree to which a test is able to truly measure what it was intended to measure
b. **reliable** – measures that provide consistent results when the experiment is repeated under exactly the same circumstances
c. **accurate** – meaning the ability to measure the variable with a sufficiently high degree of precision.

For example, your outcome measure could be the total time taken to solve 50 random mathematical puzzles of a similar difficulty correctly. Summing up the time it takes you to solve 5 puzzles might be insufficient, 200 potentially excessive.

 ### DEFINE A TREATMENT, AND STICK TO IT

To measure the impact of your treatment on the outcome variable, set a treatment protocol and stick to it. It is important to minimise the variance of any other context variable, as it will make it harder to establish a clear causality between treatment and outcome measurement. In our example, this could mean sticking to a strict 30-minute meditation protocol – meditating in the same room and at the same time of day on treatment days.

SET A TIMEFRAME

While RCTs typically run treatment and control groups at the same time, that's not possible in an n=1 experiment. You are the only subject and hence the limiting factor. That's why setting a timeframe becomes critical to ensure that a sufficient amount of data points can be generated. If your experiment only allows one measurement per day, make sure to run it for at least a few weeks.

 ## SET AN EXPERIMENTAL DESIGN

In n=1 studies, three experimental designs are most common:

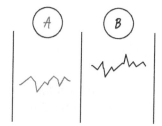

a. A–B

This is the most basic design to study causality. There are two phases: phase A, which measures the baseline without any intervention, and phase B, where the treatment is applied.

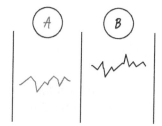

b. A–B–A

Slightly more sophisticated, this design lets you compare the changes to the outcome variable before and after the treatment. It will also help to determine the duration of the effect: increased levels in the second A phase could indicate spillovers from the previous treatment phase B.

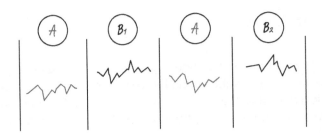

c. A–B1–A–B2
This experiment design lets you determine the effect of the *intensity* of the treatment on the outcome variable. To use our example, you might be interested in finding out if a longer meditation in the morning further boosts your outcome variable. So you could extend the 30 minutes you meditate during phase B1 to 45 minutes each morning in phase B2.

 ## CALCULATE THE DIFFERENCES

Simply take the average of each of the phases and calculate the difference to determine if your treatment (in our example, the meditation in the morning) had an effect on the measured outcome variable.

 ## DETERMINE IF THE RESULT IS SIGNIFICANT

This is the tricky mathematical part. You might have heard of the p-value, a measure for statistical significance if the variable follows a normal distribution and the sample size is large.[62]

A few words of caution. Be careful about interpretations of causality. Experiments primarily establish correlation, which should not be confused with causation. In addition, data quality and measurement can be a challenge. The quality of the results are only as good as the quality of the data you receive from your experiments. Running A–B–A and A–B–A–B tests rather than just the A–B test and comparing both of the A phases with each other is a good way to ensure a robust baseline and a sufficient quality of your outcome metric.

FURTHER EXAMPLES

Pilot plants

Changes to production processes or underlying technologies are often a risky undertaking. Even though today's software allows engineers to model and simulate changes digitally before rolling them out at scale, there are often real-life conditions that cannot be accurately be controlled for. Instead of deploying changes throughout their entire production facilities, manufacturing companies typically start with one or two pilot plants. The idea is similar to running a small-scale n=1 experiment. It allows the company to test a new production technology in real life, learning from failures and hence minimising risk.

Running quick experiments with HIT

Human intelligence tasks (HIT) are short assignments that are completed by users who are getting paid on a per-task basis. Common platforms are Amazon's Mechanical Turk, Clickworker and Toluna. These platforms are ideal to test people's reactions to advertising slogans or new logo designs. To do that, you need to specify the target group (women in their thirties with A levels), the sample size (20 people per group) and a methodology (ranking of alternatives). In contrast to the experiments outlined above which focused on observable outcomes, this method relies on survey responses. Surveys typically suffer from what is known as 'satisficing' – the tendency of the respondent to select the first reasonable response, agreeing with assertions, or even responding completely at random. Make sure to frame the question as easily as possible and keep the duration of the survey short to reduce satisficing. A forced ranking of survey answers typically yields the best results as it is a difficult cognitive task and forces absolute comparisons.

//////////// THE BOTTOM LINE ////////////

How do you know if your solution actually works? How can we make sure that our actions have the effect we intend? When it comes to understanding causal relationships, we typically revert to speculation, mimicking others or best practices. But the results often disappoint, because best practices may work in one situation but not in others. Experiments allow you to test your solutions and find out if they survive the crash with reality. Use randomised control trials (such as A/B tests) if you can randomise and have a large enough sample size for both control and treatment group. Or apply n=1 experiments for situations with only one subject.

Part 4

Complete the mission

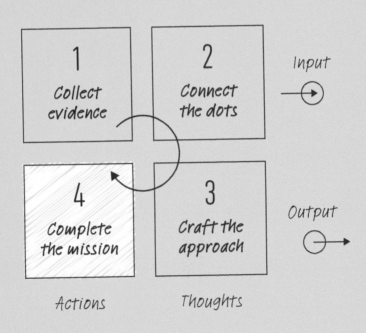

1 Collect evidence	2 Connect the dots	Input
4 Complete the mission	3 Craft the approach	Output
Actions	Thoughts	

Both of your authors are optimists by nature. But we're also realists. It's in that spirit that this final part of the book was written. We hope for success, but we plan for failure. This is rational as most efforts to change fail. The majority of company mergers fail to realise their expected value. By February, more than 80% of us have abandoned our new year's resolutions. To put it mildly, making change is really hard.

Even brilliant solutions to problems, those informed by the right data and a clear-headed understanding of causal relationships, aren't worth much if you can't put those solutions into action. In fact, the business and workplace landscape is littered with strategies that failed once organisations tried to execute them. The reasons for such failures vary. Solutions can backfire because the experts or funding needed to execute them turn out to be unavailable or far more significant than everyone expected initially. The decision that everyone agreed on ended up locking your company into a path you are desperate to find a route away from.

In the first three parts of *The Decision Maker's Playbook* we've talked about how to make smart choices. In this part, we want to share how to make that change stick, to ensure that the good choices that you make today become the winning strategies and change programmes of tomorrow.

Because execution failure is so common, it is vital for decision makers to understand what causes such failure and to master strategies for counter-acting those forces. In this fourth and final part we will examine several such strategies (including real options) and incentive systems that will motivate others to execute a solution you've settled on and best practices for implementation.

Chapter Ten

—

Multiply your possibilities

Use real options to improve your odds of success

Your task is not to foresee the future, but to enable it.
Antoine de Saint Exupéry, Citadelle or *The Wisdom of the Sands (1948)*

////// BENEFITS OF THIS MENTAL TACTIC //////

No matter if you're trying to decide whether to build a new factory, buy a car or hire a new employee, you might benefit from the ability to change your mind. This tactic is useful when you have to make decisions with major consequences under uncertainty.

In uncertain situations, it is important to be able to switch between options when circumstances change. This flexibility, of course, typically carries a cost.

This mental tactic helps you to:

- consider future 'optionality': the ability to revisit and change your decision in the future

- calculate the costs and benefits of real options

- decide in which situations it is reasonable to purchase those options

- minimise the risks of bad or incorrect decisions

- maximise the number of choices you have at relatively low cost

- think about the value of information to make better decisions.

////// USE REAL OPTIONS TO IMPROVE YOUR ODDS OF SUCCESS //////

After Annie found the perfect apartment in Edinburgh, her landlord made her an intriguing offer. If she signed a lease over 24 months (instead of 12 months, which was the typical term), she could save £500 in rent every month. Annie had good employment prospects in the city, and she and her partner were planning to stay in the region for at least the next five years. £500 off her rent of £4,000 per month for 24 months would mean a benefit of £12,000 over two years. That's a lot of money, but what if she needs to break the lease? What should Annie do?

Here we are introducing the idea of real options, a way of helping you evaluate or revisit decisions in response to changing conditions. We all make very material economic decisions, with very real trade-offs. Should we buy a house or rent? Should we purchase airline tickets today or wait to see if the price will go down next week? Should we pay a deposit for a private school for our child, knowing that we might get a new job in another part of the country next year? Should we invest in a new line in our factory even though we don't have any new client orders yet? Thinking in options will help you plan for uncertainty, and stay flexible.

//////// AN INTRODUCTION TO OPTIONS ////////

Before we dive in, let's do a quick overview of financial options.

"An option provides the holder with the right to buy or sell a specified quantity of an underlying asset at a fixed price (called a strike price or an exercise price) at or before the expiration date of the option."[63] Options are useful if you want to create certainty in your decisions. For example, you know that you will need some steel in four months' time to construct a new plant but have nowhere to store it in the meantime. Instead of buying the steel itself, you can buy the option to buy the steel *in the future* but at a price that will be fixed today. That is, you *can* buy the steel, but you don't *have* to – hence it's an option. You pay a small premium to do so, but you're buying an insurance policy that the price will increase beyond a level that you would find acceptable. In financial terms, this is referred to as a call option. The reverse of a call option is the right, but not the obligation, to sell an asset at a later date at a given price. This is referred to as a put option.

Let's go back to Annie's lease. Annie has *given up* optionality – the ability to get money back if she decides to move out before the lease expires, for a benefit of $500 per month. Should she do it? Let's take a look at her options.

In the decision tree that follows, a rectangle symbolises a decision node, whereas a circle symbolises chance node.[64]

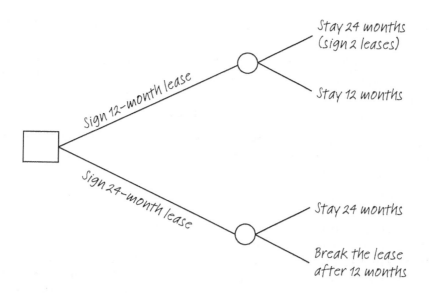

Whether or not Annie should take up the offer and choose the 2-year lease depends on her subjective probability of staying for 12 or 24 months. Let's assume she estimates the likelihood of staying for two years at 80% and one year at 20%.

		Rent	Expected rent	
Sign 12-month lease 80%	Stay 24 months (sign 2 leases)	£96,000	0.8 · £96,000 = £76,800	⎱ Σ = 86,400
20%	Stay 12 months	£48,000	0.2 · £48,000 = £9,600	
Sign 24-month lease 80%	Stay 24 months	£84,000	0.8 · £84,000 = £67,200	⎱ Σ = 84,000
20%	Break the lease after 12 months	£84,000	0.2 · £84,000 = £16,800	

With these likelihoods, Annie should indeed sign the 24-month lease as it will save her £2,400 (£86,400–£84,000). To put it a different way, Annie is being paid £12,000 over the course of 24 months in exchange for her to give up the option of leaving after 12 months. Given Annie's subjective probabilities, signing the 24-month lease will improve her situation by £2,400.

Option value not only plays a role when renting, but also when buying properties. In many jurisdictions in the USA, when buying a house or apartment, one pays a relatively small deposit (for instance, $1,000) to hold the property for, say, three days, in order to conduct the necessary due diligence. Should you decide not to buy the property, the seller gets to keep your $1,000. In that instance, you're choosing the option to buy the property at a later date at an agreed price, and preventing anyone else from buying it.

Sometimes you can obtain these options at no cost, depending on your negotiating power. Here's a trivial example. On a Saturday morning, you're out shopping for a new outfit for a party that night. You've tried on some clothes that you like in the first shop you go into (this should be a clue that Simon and Julia are old souls, we're still trying on clothes in real shops). But you don't know if they'll be your favourite as you might see any number of other terrific outfits during the day. So you ask the sales assistant to hold the items for you until 3pm, and they agree to do so. At this point, you've acquired an option – you have the right, but not the obligation, to buy those items at the price on the tags any time before 3pm on Saturday. Cleverly, you've managed to obtain this option at no cost to yourself, but at some inconvenience and risk to the store's staff and owners. They have to store the items securely for you, and politeness dictates that they don't sell them to anyone else. If you decide not to exercise your option, you simply don't return to the store and at 3:01pm, the items go back on the sales rack.

This simple example is actually the exception. Options almost never come for free. Consider the case of Alex and Danny, a couple with two children under eight. Each of them have busy full-time jobs and a variety of other commitments. Four months ago, they realised that they spent almost no time together. So, Alex proposed a creative solution that they would reserve a babysitter every Friday night. If they felt like going out to the movies or for dinner, the babysitter Matt would be on their doorstep at 7pm. But if they felt like staying in for a family dinner, and so cancelled on Matt, they would still pay him. They had to, they determined, in order to ensure that Matt would be available on the Friday nights that they did want to go out.

USING OPTIONS IN YOUR DECISION MAKING

Once you start looking, options are all around you. Understanding how to multiply and maximise your options becomes a useful tool in your decision-making arsenal. We're going to introduce three types of options that we think are particularly helpful as you make a decision: the option to expand, the option to delay and the option to abandon.

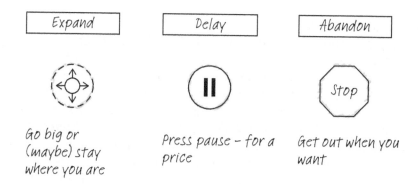

| Expand | Delay | Abandon |

Go big or (maybe) stay where you are

Press pause – for a price

Get out when you want

Option to expand

The first category is the option to expand, to effectively double or triple down on your current decision at some future point. For example, executives at a manufacturing company may not know if the company will need to expand its production facilities, but they know it would benefit by having the option to do so in the future if demand for its products increases. By purchasing additional land near its factory today, they can create the option to expand tomorrow if that turns out to be the right move. If it doesn't make sense to expand, they can simply sell the land or lease it to someone else. Options give leaders the ability, but not the obligation, to revise a decision in the future if it proves to be beneficial.

One other place you see decision makers establishing their option to expand is in the dying moments of a film, where a cliff-hanger conclusion sets up the possibility for a sequel. Take the dying scenes of Roland Emmerich's *Godzilla*. Even after the world has been saved, we fade out on the image of one of Godzilla's eggs cracking open. The world is safe . . . until the sequel.

Option to delay

The option to delay is fairly self-explanatory. It's the right to undertake a project in the future, while not committing to undertake it today. You can also think about the option to delay in relation to employment relationships.

During the 2009 global financial crisis, some professional service firms practised a variant of the option to delay in relation to their new hires. US law firm Skadden Arps had hired associates (entry-level lawyers straight out of law school) but the market for top-tier legal services had slowed to such an extent that it didn't make sense to bring these associates on board right after their graduation. However, the market hadn't slowed *so* much that it made sense to tell the associates to start looking for another job. The Skadden Arps partners were, in effect, looking to buy time. They did it by offering the would-be associates 50% of their first-year salary ($80,000 at the time) in return for starting work a year later. During that time, associates could travel or write the Great American Novel or anything else, secure in the knowledge that they would have a job at the firm in a year's time. Meanwhile, the firm could manage its payroll costs by exercising its (admittedly costly) option to delay.

Consider too the case of a film producer who reads a book that deeply moves her. She senses that this story deserves another audience and envisages that it would make a wonderful film. She buys for a fairly nominal sum (authors are not so well-paid) the rights to the movie. The producer is buying an exclusive option. She has purchased the right to make the movie, but also the right to delay making the movie until she is ready – or to never make the film. But while she holds the option, she prevents other producers from making the film.

There is another category of real options known as the option to switch. The option to switch is effectively the right to press pause on a project or commercial operation (for instance, because the political or security situation in the market deteriorated) and then to resume it again when certain conditions are met.

Option to abandon

The third category of options is the option to abandon – to withdraw your involvement in a project at a certain point, or when given conditions arise. Employment probation is one practical illustration of an option to abandon. Say Simon hires Julia as a new operator for his 3D printer. While Simon is excited about the possibilities of 3D printing, he's not sure that he can build a real business out of it. So Simon adds a clause in the employment agreement specifying a 90-day probation period, at which time the employment relationship will be evaluated and confirmed, or not, at his discretion.

Through the probation period, Simon is giving himself the option to abandon: the ability to discontinue the employment relationship at no cost to himself or his company. Temping agencies, which provide staff on short-term contracts to employers, possess similar flexibility. An option to abandon is far simpler to exercise than dismissing a traditional employee.[65]

To return to our retail examples from earlier, think about companies who offer free shipping and returns on products purchased online. The company is effectively providing you, the consumer, with a free option to abandon the products within a set period (often 30 or 60 days) if you find them unsuitable or unsatisfactory. In some cases, companies will ask you to pay for the return shipping on an item if you decide you don't want it. In exchange for the option to try the item on in the comfort of your home, or test it alongside the rest of your decor, you are effectively acquiring a put option. You are paying for the right to sell the items back to the retailer at the agreed price, minus the cost of shipping. In order to have these items in your home, you agree to accept the possibility that you might not like them enough to keep them and will have to pay to return them.

MAXIMISING OPTIONS

One of the goals of leaders should be to help organisations multiply their options – to an appropriate extent. Too many options and you can become paralysed when trying to make a decision. Too few and you may be cornered into a course of action that doesn't work for you.

The two of us give lots of advice to people early in their careers. Often, the dilemma that young people are facing is how to pick a first role (or company or industry) while they are very uncertain about their own preferences, and painfully aware of the ever-changing nature of the world of work. In such instances, we typically encourage people to think in terms of options, no matter what stage of their career they are in.

Early on, where uncertainty is high, we encourage people to maximise the number and range of their future options by taking jobs that expand future possibilities, rather than fore-closing them. This might mean, for instance, pursuing a management training programme in a large company, with opportunities to try on different roles in different functions, including finance, marketing, product development and so on. By taking on such a role, a graduate is effectively buying themselves an option to pursue a range of future careers, without fore-closing any of them.

//////// A NOTE ON BAD OPTIONS ////////

We've advocated maximising your options in a whole range of settings. We've argued that where uncertainty is high, flexibility is king. As always, this is true only to a point. There will always be bad options which are too expensive or complex to justify the effort. For us, the classic example is travel insurance. It is a costly investment, where the ability to exercise your right to compensation is typically confined to a very limited set of circumstances. Now, while travel insurance can provide financial compensation for disruptions, it cannot give you back what you probably wanted in the first place – a smooth holiday experience, or the ability to arrive at your board meeting on time. Not all options are a good deal, and not all options give you the flexibility you are seeking.

CHECKLIST

How to be smart with options

BE CLEAR ABOUT THE TYPE OF OPTIONALITY YOU ARE SEEKING

The investment approach to thinking about options is helpful in other contexts too. Be specific about the kind of optionality you are seeking, such as:

- certainty about a price or a circumstance (minimisation of the downside risk of price increases)

- the ability to wait and make a decision at some point in the future

- the ability to cease a new project if it just isn't working.

DETERMINE WHAT YOU'RE PREPARED TO PAY FOR CERTAINTY AND FLEXIBILITY

Knowing that you want an option is only half the battle. Determining what you might be prepared to pay for optionality is the other half, and what someone is prepared to pay to extend that flexibility to you. $1,000 might be a very reasonable sum to buy a house in three days. $1 million might be the price to keep the land next to your factory empty for five years, before you can decide whether to build on it.

USE A COSTS AND BENEFITS TREE TO ROBUSTLY ESTIMATE THE TOTAL COST – AND THE VALUE OF YOUR OPTION

Real options are conceptually much more than mere alternatives – they are a way to place a quantitative value on those alternatives. Once you've generated your options, draw them out and assign values.

PUSH YOURSELF TO ENSURE THAT THE OPTIONS OR INSURANCE YOU'RE TAKING ON ARE REALLY WORTH IT

There are some instances where the options we take out are not worth it. Overpriced insurance is a classic example. Taking on extra staff to prepare for a rush that may not arise is another. Waiting around for a better job offer that may never materialise is a third. You can ask yourself:

- Would I truly exercise this option?

- If the event I am insuring against never arose, would I still be happy I had the insurance?

If the event *did* arise, would the insurance be sufficient to compensate me? In the case of travel insurance, for instance, the payout might be enough to get you where you are going, but can't repair a missed vacation – so perhaps the money does not matter.

//////////// FURTHER EXAMPLES ////////////

Buy or rent?

When you start to look, you will see options all around. The choice to buy or rent is one such example. Let's assume we have a would-be householder who could afford to either rent or buy the home of her choosing. When she rents, she gives up the ability to control the property and to earn capital gains if it appreciates in value for the flexibility to leave the property in the near future – the option to abandon – if it doesn't suit her needs. Let's say she goes one step further and takes out a month-to-month lease. She potentially pays a little more but is free to leave the apartment with just 30 days' notice if conditions change.

Flight or flex?

The often mysterious world of airline pricing is replete with options. If you purchase the lowest-cost fare, you are often giving up all of your options in exchange for a cheaper ticket. This includes the option to delay (by moving your flight to another day or time) and the option to abandon (by cancelling your flight for a refund). Buying a flexible fare gives you back these options – for a price.

Some airlines provide what is known as a seat guarantee for their most frequent flyers. The guarantee represents a promise that the frequent flyer will be able to obtain a seat on any of the airline's flights, including full ones. They are effectively giving you a permanent option to acquire a seat on any of their flights as a thank you for your loyalty – and all of your previous (and, they hope, future) spending. You'll notice that exercising this option is likely to result in another passenger without this option being summarily ejected from the flight.

Mind the gap (year)

US President Barack Obama's eldest daughter Malia made headlines in 2016, when the White House announced that she would be taking a gap year before commencing university study. A gap year – where young people might travel, work, or volunteer – can be seen as an option to delay. The student's university of choice gives the student the right to be admitted a year later than they would have otherwise planned (also an option to delay). In this case, the option is rather one-sided – the student still has the option to try to be admitted to a different university on the same timeframe or even to decide that continuing to study isn't for her at all and exercise the option to abandon at no cost.

THE BOTTOM LINE

Having the option (but not the obligation) to act in the future is valuable, particularly in environments that change quickly and unpredictably, and that are hard to shape or influence. Options are everywhere you look. Understanding and valuing options is an important skill to hedge for future contingencies. Your goal should be to create and use them wisely to enable optimal decision making in the future. Remember, a truly valuable option hardly ever comes for free. Start thinking about your future choices as today's options, each with a value attached.

Chapter Eleven

Engineer incentives

Energise everyone to be their best

Show me the incentive and I will show you the outcome.
Charlie Munger

///// BENEFITS OF THIS MENTAL TACTIC /////

Misaligned incentives are one of the biggest sources of organisational and relationship dysfunction. If you want to achieve great things, make sure you align everyone's incentives.

The takeaway: your interests are not the same as other people's interests, and no one cares about your interests as much as you. We've talked a lot so far about *what* to do – to articulate and frame your problems and identify and implement the right tools. Here we turn to the *how* questions that will allow you to get big things done. To accomplish your mission, understanding incentives is fundamental.

//// ENERGISE EVERYONE TO BE THEIR BEST ////

Your friend and their spouse have not been getting along for several years. There are no climactic arguments, just thinly veiled contempt that's accumulated over decades of proximity. Your friend visits a lawyer for some advice about whether they should commence divorce proceedings or seek couples therapy. The lawyer notes that divorce proceedings will be drawn out and very expensive, but strongly recommends that your friend pursue this course.

You are selling your house and it's on the market for $400,000. The first weekend that it is on the market, you receive an offer for $395,000 and are aware that there may be an offer from another party for $415,000, but that it will take a few weeks for the would-be buyer to make the offer. Your agent strongly recommends that you take the $395,000 offer.

You are the CEO of a major pharmaceutical corporation on the verge of retirement, and your compensation package is linked to the company's share price performance. You become aware of the negative results of trials of your company's newest drug. You can decide whether to disclose these negative results now, or have the next CEO do so in six months' time, but you are fully aware that investors (not to mention doctors and patients) would benefit from knowing now that the drug is unlikely to be successful. You stall – the announcement becomes the next leader's problem.

These three cases are all instances of misaligned incentives. Your lawyer doesn't get paid if you get back together with your spouse; your estate agent takes such a relatively small percentage of the overall purchase price that they'd rather accept the lower offer than wait around a few more weeks for you to make a lot more money; what's good for the pharmaceutical CEO isn't what's good for the investors or the company. A look at any organisation or relationship will reveal a misalignment in incentives somewhere. The problem – this misalignment can be extremely costly for at least one party and, over time, reduces trust, cooperation and the ability to get things done.

WHAT TO LOOK FOR: TWO BIG MISALIGNMENTS

Two categories of misalignment are the source of much of the organisational dysfunction you see around you: moral hazard and principal-agent problems.[66]

Moral hazard

What risks would you take if you knew there were limited negative consequences for you? The answer to that question encapsulates the problem of moral hazard: we take more risks when we feel protected from the consequences. As an example, you might be a little more careless about leaving a phone or a laptop on a table in a coffee shop if you know you have insurance against theft, or if the device belongs to an employer who will readily replace it.

The subprime mortgage crisis which engulfed the USA and eventually global financial markets from 2007 onwards is a larger example of this phenomenon. In retrospect, it was easy to see that many borrowers would be unlikely to be able to repay their loans. For the originators of the loans themselves, as well as the financial institutions that bundled them on to complex derivative products known as mortgage-backed securities, this risk didn't matter too much. For many years, there were willing buyers of these loans and plenty of opportunity for the originators and bundlers to make a substantial return. For the individual Wall Street trader dealing in these instruments, their downside was strictly capped. At worst, they would lose their jobs, and at best they stood to make an enormous financial return. The systematic risk that these instruments created did not concern them – it was not factored in to their incentives.[67]

When people are protected from the downsides of their behaviour, and have the opportunity to enjoy a meaningful benefit, moral hazard will persist.

Principal-agent problem

A principal-agent problem arises when one person or entity (the agent) is allowed to act on behalf of another person (the principal). It seems sensible that the agent would have the principal's best interests at heart in such a situation and would act accordingly. However, agents frequently have various competing pressures that prevent them from doing so. For instance, is a financial advisor recommending products offered by their institution versus another because it genuinely is the best product for the client, or because they will receive an additional commission for doing so?[68]

In our example above, is the lawyer urging divorce proceedings because they stand to gain financially from advising on a formal separation? It's almost impossible to know, even for the lawyer themselves. But, once we understand incentives, we have an opportunity to design them more effectively.

Imagine for a moment that you have a choice between becoming an investment banker (with a starting salary of $100,000 plus a bonus) and a salesperson (with a starting salary of $60,000 plus a bonus).

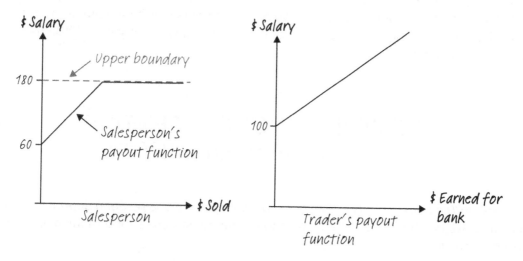

Not surprisingly, it is more attractive at face-value to be a banker – after all, your fixed salary is $40,000 higher. Now let's look at the bonus element (what some organisations call 'performance incentives'). The salesperson's bonus is capped as they can never make more than twice their starting salary. Commission caps make some sense in that they prevent commissions from eating *too far* into profits. But they can also be counter-productive. Let's say that this particular salesperson is particularly persuasive and efficient and by September has earned $120,000 in commissions. For the last quarter of the year, they have to keep coming into work, or they'll stop earning their salary. But they also have no incentive to call a single customer, cultivate a new relationship or make an additional sale.

Now consider our investment banker. Like our salesperson, they earn their $100,000 salary no matter what, provided they keep coming into the office. But their bonus has no cap, and is linked to the short-term performance of their own investments and those of the company overall. Even worse, from an incentive perspective, a very large part of her success will be a function of luck and timing within the overall economic cycle. In such a case, the banker's incentive is to take larger and larger risks – the downside is capped and their upside is theoretically enormous. The worst thing that could happen to our banker is that they earn £0 as a bonus – unlikely, and still not a very bad outcome considering they are guaranteed to earn $100,000.

The financial markets overall have a preference for stability: making sound, long-term investments and ensuring the smooth and efficient flow of capital. But the incentive structure for many of the actors in the system is completely at odds with this objective. Indeed, the misalignment of incentives and the desire for short-term performance above long-term stability has been identified as one of the contributing factors behind the 2008/9 global financial crisis. The phenomenon of packaging investments which paid big up-front fees, while ultimately creating longer-term losses even had its own acronym – IBGYBG (I'll be gone, you'll be gone).

DESIGNING YOUR INCENTIVE SCHEME PROPERLY

As always in *The Decision Maker's Playbook,* we want to help you respond appropriately to the challenges we identify. Here, we are going to lay out our structure for designing appropriate incentive schemes.

INCENTIVE	WHEN TO USE	EXAMPLE SITUATION
Financial reward (e.g. performance-based bonus)	When the desired outcome is measurable and can be correlated to the size of the reward, and when there's limited inherent motivation (people would not do it for free)	• Sales from cold calling
Financial penalty (e.g. fine or docked pay for non-performance or rule-breaking)	When the desired outcome is measurable and can be correlated to the size of the penalty; when loss aversion will be motivating but the risk of backlash is minimal; and when penalty is socially accepted	• Maintaining safety behaviours in a plant • Team's bonus pool that is reduced each time the penalised behaviour is observed
Non-material rewards (e.g. video game points)	When the desired outcome is measurable and can be correlated to a points scheme; when financial incentivisation is too costly or socially inappropriate	• Fitness challenges and online learning modules • Donations and sponsorship tiers
Social proof (e.g. praise and recognition)	When the desired outcome is difficult to measure or correlate to any reward; insufficient intrinsic motivation (people would not do it without recognition)	• Participating in office extra-curriculars (e.g. organising the holiday party)
Identity coherence (e.g. connecting the desired behaviour to the person's best sense of themselves)	When the desired outcome is difficult to measure or correlate to any reward; intrinsic motivation is high (people would do it for free and without recognition)	• Mentoring and championing younger staff

CHECKLIST

How to break down incentives

 ANALYSE INDIVIDUAL'S INCENTIVES AND LOOK FOR SIGNS OF NON-ALIGNMENT

What are people incentivised to do? Are the incentives aligned with those they are cooperating with? Are there ways that allow them to 'game the system'?

 TAKE ADVANTAGE OF LOSS AVERSION

Human beings are much more sensitive to the possibility of loss than the opportunity for gain.[69] For instance, bonuses might be structured by telling the sales team that they have been awarded the maximum bonus on 1 January and that deductions will be made for lost clients or failure to meet targets.

 IDENTIFY DIFFERENT OPTIONS TO USE THE SAME RESOURCES

For instance, how much of an employee's pay should be variable based on performance (such as the product reaching the customer on time)? What metrics would you use? How do you avoid misalignment?

GOODHART'S LAW

We have seen that incentives can be reframed in ways that help us make a clear-eyed assessment of the situation. But what about situations where your incentives, no matter how well-intentioned, miss the mark entirely? Named after the Governor of the Bank of England who coined the phrase, Goodhart's law refers to a situation where measuring a phenomenon causes performance to be distorted so much that the measure ceases to be useful. Or, as Goodhart himself put it: "When a measure becomes a target, it ceases to be a good measure."[70]

Driving the snakes out of India

To illustrate, let's look at how the British tried to drive snakes out of India. The governing authority of the country confronted an infestation of cobras, including in major cities. This was obviously undesirable and the British turned to a predictable solution – bounty. Indian subjects would be paid for each dead cobra they could present to the authorities. On the face of it, this approach makes sense: you engage your community in shared ownership of the problem, you give them an incentive to reduce it and you require evidence (in this case, a handful of dead cobras) to demonstrate that the change has actually taken place.

In this case, as in many others, the policy actually produced the opposite of the desired change. In the end, there were many more cobras in India than in the beginning.

How and why? People responded to the outcome (produce a dead cobra) and the incentive (get some money) by changing the input – the enterprising subjects of the British Empire started breeding more cobras. This of course made it even easier for them to collect their incentives, but completely perverted the ultimate goal of the British policy. Realising the situation that they had created was untenable, the British ended the policy of paying bounties, but again trapped themselves with misaligned incentives. They had the same input problem (too many cobras) and their desired outcome was the same (more dead cobras), but the incentive had now switched (no cash for cobras). As a result, people did stop breeding cobras, but they also released all the cobras in their possession, thus compounding the original problem that the British had set out to solve.

By now, you can probably identify multiple examples in your organisations and teams of how these kinds of incentive problems arise. It might be the strict policy that requires workers to be at their desks until 5.30pm, but makes no distinction between the staff member assisting one more client and the employee shopping online for Halloween costumes for his pet. It might be the compensation structure that pays sales people huge bonuses for signing up a new customer, but doesn't create any incentives for maintaining the relationship beyond the first sale.

WHY RATIONAL INCENTIVES FAIL

This is the point at which some of us despair. We throw up our hands and declare that all incentives are hopelessly misaligned, measuring things only makes it worse, and there are snakes everywhere. What can we do? One thing we definitely can do in a complicated world is to begin to take a good look at human behaviour and understand how people are motivated to take action.

The pizza, the money and the text message

To do that, we need to switch from India under the British Empire to present-day Israel in a semiconductor factory. Dan Ariely, a renowned behavioural economist at Duke in the USA (whose lab has the best name we've ever heard for a research institution: The Center for Advanced Hindsight) and bosses everywhere were keen to understand how to motivate production-line workers to increase productivity – to produce more in the same amount of time.[71] Ariely divided the workers into four groups:

- A control group (more on them later) – they kept working as they had been.
- A group that was offered a pizza voucher when certain targets were achieved, on the assumption that we are highly motivated by free food.
- A group who received a cash bonus for achieving certain performance targets.
- A group who received a text message with a word of congratulation (good job" or "nice work") from a supervisor at the end of the day if targets were achieved.

Take a moment and make a prediction. Which groups increased their productivity? Which group's productivity increased the most? One school of thought would suggest that the third group's productivity should increase the most because people are responsive to monetary incentives. Assuming that the factory workers could increase their output more, they would do so. Pizza might work a little bit (because by eating free pizza, perhaps you don't have to pay for lunch). But it should work a bit less well than cash, on the basis that not everyone likes pizza and not everyone likes pizza all the time.

Here's what really happened. Pizza was the most successful motivator on the first day (maybe we do all love a free lunch). However, after a week, the strongest motivator was the congratulations text from a boss – beating the pizza and the cash.

There are a couple of things to love about this neatly designed study.[72] First, it demonstrates that we are powerfully social creatures: we are extremely motivated by feedback from others, and it shapes our performance. Second, incentives even in an employment context, and even on a production line, may have nothing to do with cold hard cash or raw numbers. Instead, we can incentivise performance in others purely via recognition and appreciation. Third, we sometimes fall into the trap of thinking that incentives and motivation must be zero-sum games – they involve a transfer of resources (often money) from an employer to an employee.

Much time, effort and worry is invested in designing incentive schemes that an organisation believes will enable it to maximise performance and productivity with the smallest amount of incentives payment. Ariely's study demonstrates that incentives (in this case, praise) can be completely free or extremely low-cost. And praise like this can actually maintain alignment of incentives over the long term:

- Business owners have an incentive to ensure that management is paying attention to performance, while also minimising the costs of creating that performance.

- Managers are nudged to pay attention to who is performing, but also to explicitly identify and appreciate that good performance.

- Employees have an incentive to demonstrate to management that they are achieving their targets on a consistent basis, and an emotional desire to be seen and appreciated.

CHECKLIST

How to turn irrational incentives to your advantage

 ### SMS SOME PRAISE TODAY

This is one of our easiest tactics to deploy, with the highest payback. Pick up your phone (we know it's close by) and text someone with your appreciation. As we've seen, it doesn't need to be complex or detailed. Try: "I value what you bring to this organisation", "I am grateful to have you on our team and just wanted you to know" or "Thank you for everything you do."

 ### MAKE IT A HABIT

Add a note to your calendar to text one person every day expressing your appreciation. Perhaps you work on a small team and are concerned you'll repeat yourself? Don't worry about it, remember Ariely's factory workers. The messages keep working over time.

 ### TRAIN YOUR TEAMS

We are fond of suggesting that if you invested an hour a year in training for all your managers, it should be in learning to give clear, authentic and regular praise. Can you set aside an hour to do this with your team? Can you propose it to a leader in your organisation?

A FINAL NOTE ON EXTRINSIC MOTIVATION

As if snakes and pizza weren't enough, we want to sound one final note of caution about using incentives to create extrinsic motivation. Extrinsic motivation is the kind that is driven by external rewards: money or fame are two good examples. Intrinsic motivation, as the name suggests, comes from within. We are intrinsically motivated to do things because it satisfies us personally. Intrinsically motivated behaviours are the kind we would do no matter what other people thought. It is often easier to practise intrinsically motivated behaviours because we want very deeply to do them. They can also often be complicated behaviours (helping others, persisting with difficult or complex tasks).

As leaders, it can be tempting to layer on additional extrinsic motivation to encourage people to do something. It can be particularly tempting when you need quick results: "We need more senior managers to mentor junior women," or "We must have people spending more time doing advanced and complex testing of our software." We have a tendency to underestimate other people's levels of intrinsic motivation and instead assume that we will have to pay them to take action on this type of challenge. But just like us, other people are also motivated by the desire to do a good job, or have interesting challenges and positive relationships at work.[73]

In fact, a meta-analysis (a type of academic mega-study, where authors combine as many studies as possible on a particular topic and try to make sense of them) warns against this. Psychologist Edward L. Deci and 2 of his colleagues analysed 128 studies and made the following observations:[74]

- Offering monetary rewards can undermine our motivation for intrinsically rewarding tasks (something we find personally satisfying such as completing a difficult puzzle or giving advice). This is called a 'crowding-out' effect.

- This crowding-out effect is strongest for complex cognitive tasks – the kinds of things that take lots of mental effort, but can be highly worthwhile.

- Symbolic rewards (such as gifts or company awards) don't have a crowding-out effect in the same way that monetary rewards do. Symbolic rewards may actually improve intrinsic motivation.

- The crowding-out effect is largest when the external rewards are significant (a big year-end bonus), are perceived as a way to control behaviour, require that the task is performed in a very specific way, or are associated with deadlines, surveillance or threats.

THE BOTTOM LINE

Incentives are tools to motivate individuals to perform actions. Misaligned incentives are one of the major causes of conflict and lost productivity in our world. However, careful up-front thought about the desired outcome, the relevant inputs and incentive system design can help anticipate and avoid common issues such as moral hazard, principal-agent and coordination problems. Pay attention to ineffective incentive systems and remember that intrinsic motivations may help you to change performance for the better, and for longer.

Chapter Twelve

Make it happen

Anticipate, execute and improve

Imagination means nothing without doing.
Charlie Chaplin's manuscript notes

BENEFITS OF THIS MENTAL TACTIC

All of the good work you've done up until now will be for nothing if you cannot execute effectively. This mental tactic – planning, structuring and executing your work effectively will help you turn ideas into reality.

We hope that this guide will be useful when you are:

- setting goals for the new year (or the new week, or the new day)
- starting a new project
- creating shared objectives for a team
- trying to bring a project back on track
- reflecting about a completed project or task.

ANTICIPATE, EXECUTE AND IMPROVE

Every year, many adults in many countries complete their tax return. It is a small, annoying project that simply must get done. We do this yearly, so we should have a rough sense of how long it takes us, right? Wrong! One researcher found that it took individuals around a week longer than they estimated to file their tax return. It is not that the individuals in the study misremembered how long it took them last year – indeed, they recalled their previous experience quite accurately. They were just irrationally optimistic that this year would be different. The tax return case is an example of a failure to execute: the inability to do what we should, when we know we should, within a reasonable timeframe. It is also an example of the *planning fallacy* – a mental bias that gets in the way of making things happen.

MAKING IT HAPPEN ONE STEP AT A TIME

We have talked about how to align incentives in order to ensure that all parties are moving in the same direction. Earlier on, we discussed the importance of using agile and experimental approaches to validate your ideas and test assumptions about possible approaches. Now we want to empower you with a few different tools to actually make big things happen.

What we want to do here is a little different. We hope that at this point you're inspired and energised to put the tools we've shared with you so far into practice in your life and work. Here, we're sharing the techniques that have worked well for us and countless peers and colleagues in terms of making change happen. Combined, these forces create what we call an 'improvement loop'.

- Pre-action – getting ready to make change happen by dodging the planning fallacy, making effective pre-commitments and identifying a critical path for action.

- Taking action – managing your work to make change happen.

- After action – reflecting on your work so you can do better next time.

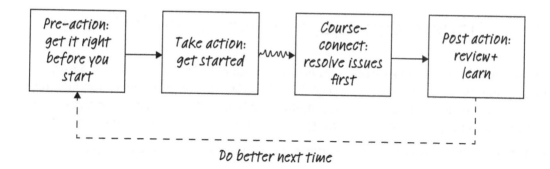

Do better next time

Pre-action – getting ready to do good

Many, perhaps most, of our efforts to make change fail. This is true for personal efforts, like New Year's resolutions, as well as for organisation-wide efforts to transform companies. The reasons are many and complex, but a common cause is a lack of preparation. You can increase the odds of success by preparing effectively. Of course, there are a variety of tools and planners that will help you. If you've picked up this book, you probably already have a few systems and tricks that work for you. We want to offer you a few of the lesser-known ideas that we think deserve a wider audience.

The first step to developing and executing successful plans is to remember that your plans are likely to be too optimistic. Here we meet the planning fallacy again. We are overconfident about our ability to make changes, and about the speed at which we can do so. It is why on 1 January we set out to lose 20 pounds by Valentine's day, or to develop a new product for our teams in one week. We actually love the planning fallacy. It reflects the optimism of the human spirit. But it holds us back too – it causes deadlines to be missed and projects to be delivered over-budget. It can lead to disappointment and frustration. Recall our tax return story from a moment ago? What can you do to prevent yourself being thwarted by the planning fallacy?

You can overcompensate: estimate how long something is likely to take you and add a (large) buffer. Since the fallacy was first identified in 1979 by Amos Tversky and Daniel Kahneman,[75] research has demonstrated that it's virtually impossible to avoid the planning fallacy. It *will* happen to you at one point or another. So, instead, if you estimate that it might take you one week to design the new market study, try doubling it.

Understand and visualise the critical path

One of the most valuable execution tools is understanding the critical path of a project. A project typically consists of a number of different activities, many of which run in parallel in that you can make progress on them simultaneously. In order to keep the original deadline for the overall project, it helps to understand the critical path. To do it, first map out:

- all the items that simply must be done in order for the project to be completed
- the order in which they must be completed
- the estimated amount of time each task will take, including waiting time.

How do you find the critical path? It is the (parallel) path that takes longest to complete. Take the construction of a house, for example.

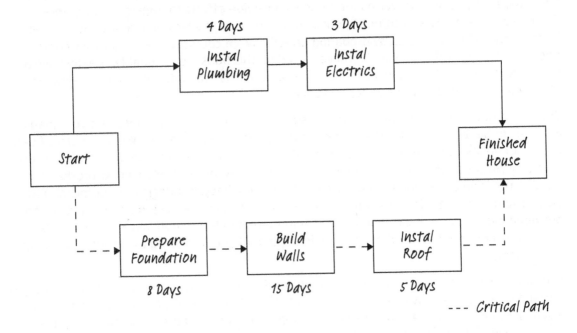

The critical path diagram allows you to see the critical path as the one that takes the longest, thereby allowing you to estimate the overall project time from start to finish (in the above case, 28 days). This way, it helps you prioritise.

Pay particular attention to long lead-time activities – those activities that need to be started early because they will take substantial time to arrange or coordinate, even if the actual effort required is not substantial. Tackle these earlier in the project timeline to avoid delays for the whole project. For example, make sure you first call the civil engineers so that they can start preparing the foundations. It wouldn't help much to liaise with the plumber or the electrician first: those activities are not on the critical path, and delaying them would have no detrimental effect on the overall timeline.

Taking action – the pre-mortem

So, you've designed your critical path, you've assigned the resourcing and responsibility and it is the night before the project is due to kick off. What do you do? You think about failure, of course! One of the things that distinguishes our most successful projects from our less successful ones (and our most successful colleagues from our less successful ones) is an obsessive attention to what could go wrong. For even the smallest project, we encourage a pre-mortem – a systematic consideration of the factors that could cause the project to fail.

For our pre-mortems, we use the following questions by forecasting forward a few months to the project failing:

- What went wrong?
- What was the first warning sign that all was not well?
- What was the second warning sign that all was not well?
- Who tried to warn us?
- Why were the signs missed? Were we too busy, too optimistic, under too much pressure?

It is helpful to do this yourself. But as you'll remember from Part 1, we often get too attached to ideas and projects just because they are ours. It is even better if you can have a trusted friend or advisor do this for you, or a leader in a completely different part of your organisation.

Manage to the plan

Preparing your critical path helps you figure out what to do. But sometimes you need some help in making sure that you actually do it. We find it very helpful to separate the doers from the trackers. For almost any effort that's important, it is useful to establish a Programme

Management Office (PMO). Of all the big ideas we have shared, this one might sound the least glamorous, but it's critically important. A PMO deliberately tracks the performance of a project or effort and provides both an objective view of performance, while also suggesting where and how to improve. Basically, a PMO's job is to be able to answer the following questions at any moment:

- Are we achieving our plan? That is, are we on time today and do we expect to be on time at the end?

- Are we using our resources appropriately? That is, are we on or under budget?

- What's coming up next and what could hurt us? That is, where are we at risk?

Note that the PMO is typically not responsible for *doing* any of the things described in the plan. And that's precisely the point. They provide a measure of independence and accountability precisely because they are not the doers. In a large organisation or a major project, you might find a PMO full of business analysts and change management experts and financial accountants. But it doesn't have to be so intensive.

Your PMO can be one person, or just part of a person's role. What *is* critical is that you establish them as the objective truth-teller, empowered to gather data and develop the answers to the above three questions. Here is a very simplified version of our tracker for the first two parts of *The Decision Maker's Playbook*.

CHAPTER	PROGRESS UPDATE	NEXT ACTION	DUE DATE FOR NEXT ACTION	DAYS UNTIL NEXT DEADLINE	RESPONSIBLE
0	Second draft done	Perform final edit	1 October	+11	Simon
1	Preliminary research done	Prepare initial outline	15 September	–5 (overdue)	Julia
2	Initial outline done	Prepare first draft	25 September	+5	Julia
3	Final edit complete	N/A: ready for publishing	–		Simon
4	First draft complete	Prepare second draft	30 September	+10	Julia
5	Initial outline done	Prepare first draft	17 October	+26	Simon

What you'll notice in this case is that the PMO isn't a person, it's just a tool. Simon and I were monitoring ourselves in real time to ensure we had visibility over everything that was happening. You can see that on this single page we can see immediately what is done (Chapter Three), what the current status and next actions are for all chapters, as well as identify areas where we are behind (Chapter One) and activities where we are close to the deadline and need to ensure we are investing enough effort in the days ahead (Chapter Two).

Create space for reflection

After you've put our action plan into place – for yourself or your team – and you have started to get consistent, predictable results, it is tempting to think that the job is done. But really effective decision makers and problem solvers don't stop there. They take one additional step.

Look backwards: the disciplined decision processes

As we noted in the beginning of this book, running robust analyses before making a decision is a good starting point. But your expectation should be that the quality of your analyses will improve over time. The way to ensure that this happens is to apply the same discipline to learning from your decisions as you do to making those decisions in the first place. None of us can ever control everything, nor will a decision maker ever have all of the knowledge that they would like in order to make a decision. Decision audits help you to take a systematic look backwards at successes and failures, and to make sense of the drivers of each. As Marcia Blenko and her colleagues wrote in *Harvard Business Review*, "Ultimately, a company's value is just the sum of the decisions it makes and executes."[76]

A high-stakes decision audit: morbidity and mortality conferences

Few professions make as many high-stakes decisions as often as medical professionals. Each new patient presents a slew of decisions: what questions to ask, which answers to believe, which tests to run, what procedures to recommend, whether to admit the patient to hospital or send them home, when and whether to consult a doctor from another specialty, what diagnosis to make.

Doctors are also human and they make mistakes sometimes with grave consequences. When such mistakes occur, the medical profession has developed a specific forum for reflection on such events. It's called the Morbidity and Mortality Conference (M&M), and it's a place where doctors gather, present a case in which the outcome was adverse to the patient, and through discussion and analysis, seek to learn from it. The practice is now heavily enshrined, particularly in large teaching hospitals.

Vinay Prasad writes of the M&M conference in the *British Medical Journal*: "Philosophically, the conference can be understood as a forum to pose the eternal question that faces any doctor who, despite his or her best efforts, encounters an adverse outcome: could I have done things differently?".[77]

The same objective should be the basis for decision audits in any field. The higher the stakes, the more important it is to make space for reflection. But we have found that these techniques are useful for decisions of almost any consequence.

To move far away from the operating theatre and the emergency room, reflection still exerts a powerful force. A study of call centre workers undergoing a training programme found that staff who spent 15 minutes at the end of the day reflecting on and writing about what they had learned that day performed 23% better when tested than those who had not reflected. One of the keys to making good decisions is reflecting on past decisions.[78]

Making decision audits work for you

Most of us don't make life or death decisions on a daily basis. But we all make decisions with consequences – and we all assume responsibility, whether for someone else's money, for a project's outcome, or for a team's performance. In conducting decision audits, we suggest using the following checklist.

CHECKLIST

How to look back on your decisions

 WOULD WE STILL MAKE THE SAME DECISION TODAY THAT WE MADE AT THE TIME?

If yes, why?

_____

 IF NOT, WHAT SPECIFIC ELEMENT OF THE ANALYSIS IS DIFFERENT?

- Were costs larger than expected? Were benefits smaller than expected?
- How could these variations in the analysis have been discovered at the time of the original decision? ("We should have requested binding quotes from necessary vendors before proceeding to avoid cost overrun" or "The variations could not have been anticipated – the 2019 zombie apocalypse put an unexpected dampener on the restaurant industry in our city.")

_____

 DID OTHERS PURSUE SIMILAR DECISIONS IN SIMILAR CIRCUMSTANCES?

What results did they achieve?

_____

 WHAT CHANGES SHOULD WE MAKE TO OUR DECISION-MAKING *ANALYSES* BASED ON THIS DECISION?

For example, "We should use ranges instead of specific numbers when estimating the future price of inputs."

_____

WHAT CHANGES SHOULD WE MAKE TO OUR DECISION-MAKING *PROCESSES* BASED ON THIS DECISION?

For example, "We will always present a do nothing option to the board" and "We would have been better off leaving the money in the bank instead of investing in vintage typewriters."

 CAN WE BE OPEN AND TRANSPARENT?

Especially when the result of a decision audit is unfavourable, it's uncomfortable but extremely valuable to share the outcome. This is how the entire organisation learns.

THE BOTTOM LINE

Big things don't just happen. But with a little pre-planning, attention to action and post-action reflection, your most important projects can fall into place. The ability to plan and execute is a learned skill – it improves over time and with practice. Teams, individuals and groups increase their odds of success by putting in place techniques to plan effectively, execute well and reflect appropriately, such as the critical-path method, the pre-mortem and the decision audit.

Chapter Thirteen
—

Conclusion

Where to from here?

*The first rule is that you've got to have multiple models –
because if you just have one or two that you're using, the
nature of human psychology is such that you'll torture
reality so that it fits your models ...*

*And the models have to come from multiple disciplines
because all the wisdom of the world is not to be found in
one little academic department.*

Charlie Munger[79]

WHERE TO FROM HERE?

We started working on *The Decision Maker's Playbook* in 2014. It was in that year that Google acquired DeepMind, a leading Artificial Intelligence company. Two years later, algorithms dethroned the incumbent Go champion, and social-media technology platforms arguably played a pivotal role in the outcome of the US presidential election.

In recent decades, the environments in which we work and live have changed tremendously. A hundred years ago, even if you lived in affluent societies, your options were limited. You could only be hired by a handful employers, limited further by the number of companies and the distance required to commute to work. Labour-saving technologies were fairly basic. You almost certainly married someone who grew up in the same town or region as yourself.[80]

By the end of the twentieth century and into the new millennium, the opposite is true. We have too many options, and our major decision problems are centered on how to make the best choices given the range of possibilities. Enter any department store and you are overwhelmed by the sheer variety of different brands. Take Amazon, which stocks more than 500 million different products. A well-educated and mobile young professional can work in large international companies or organisations and start a family with someone who grew up 12,000 miles away from her. In this environment, making sense of these challenges requires a set of tools to help us reduce, focus and decide which among the countless options are the most useful.

THE AGE OF ALGORITHMIC DECISION MAKING

Today, algorithms and digital systems have come to the rescue and to help us make choices. They do this in a number of ways, but they primarily use our past behaviour and the revealed preferences of people similar to us to help filter our options. Take a review platform such as TripAdvisor. It's nothing new that we follow the advice of our friends and visit the restaurant that most of them recommend. But the internet has made it orders of magnitudes easier to share and aggregate data such as reviews or recommendations. So even though we theoretically have many options, we end up booking the restaurant on top of the list.

Soon the world will be dominated by algorithms which predict fairly accurately what we want, prefer and do next. The more data these algorithms gather, the better their predictions will become. It's not science fiction to suggest that, in the near future, algorithms will know which of our mental (and emotional) buttons to press in order to make us believe, want or do things. In itself, this is not necessarily bad. After all, we use these algorithms voluntarily because they offer us some kind of benefit. They take some load off our shoulders to sift through options and present us with the most suitable ones –or they present the pieces of information that we are most likely to latch on to. And they don't have to do that perfectly. It's enough for them to simply be *better* than what we can come up with ourselves. Google Maps' routing feature occasionally leads us to blocked streets and we need to take a detour. But in the overwhelming majority of cases, it leads us the along the most time-efficient paths, saving us hours, days or even weeks of lifetime.

Remember the incentive systems from earlier in this book? It's not hard to see that incentives may not be fully aligned. From the perspective of their owners, algorithms are tools to accomplish a goal, such as selling services or keeping us on a website so we can be exposed to ads. In solving these goals, such as profit maximisation, algorithms serve us suggestions, such as nuggets of news that are designed to stir outrage and polarisation. They may not be in line with the goals we set for ourselves if we are open-minded and weigh evidence of either side to form a balanced opinion. Our dependency on algorithms can make us subject to manipulation.

The more we use digital systems, the more data is collected. The more data collected, the better algorithmic models can be trained, and the more powerful the algorithms get. The more powerful these algorithms become, the more we delegate our decision-making authority to them. And this is where the problem lies. In doing so, we give up part of our autonomy, and we become dependent on algorithms. We become vulnerable against big tech, which is – thanks to large-scale effects of data – increasing the concentration of information and making it harder for us to opt out or switch. Just as Google Maps is better than a taxi driver at selecting the fastest route, we surrender to algorithms for much more important decisions: what we read, who we date, or who we vote for.

We are highlighting the potentially dangerous aspects of technology here, and the problems that are related to it: technological dependence, safety, biases, intransparency or 'black boxes'. We don't talk about the tremendous welfare gain that algorithms such as search engines have generated in the fields of logistics or healthcare. These achievements are clearly laudable, but they don't take away from the risks.

Mental tactics as presented in this book serve not only as effective tools, but also as means to reflect on our preconceptions, beliefs and biases. Taking this meta view can be an antidote, a shield against being hacked by algorithms.[81] Even when we are still in the last instance of decision making (in autonomous systems, this is called 'human in the loop'), we surrender our authority *de facto* to machines. While we still have the possibility to override the suggestions made by algorithms, we typically don't do it.

Thinking and decision making have got some serious competition: machine algorithms. Your individual set of mental tactics serve as a check, back-up and corrective so that you can maintain your independence and critical thinking.

A MAP OF THE TERRITORY

Mental tactics, as you by now are aware, are models that aim to explain parts of reality, and provide a decision framework that helps you make better choices and drive the outcomes you intend. They are maps that aim to describe the territory (reality).[82] A seafarer uses a map to locate his current position using various navigational instruments, dead reckoning (a navigational method calculating the current position based on known previous locations) and a triangulation of landmarks (mountain tops, harbours, buildings on land). He uses a map as a simplified copy of reality to simulate his position, and continuously compares the map against the observed reality.

Maps are necessarily reductionist. They de-emphasise data (observations or evidence) that isn't relevant for the specific decision situation (many nautical maps don't show elevations), and instead direct our focus and attention towards data that is relevant such as water depth. This is necessary, as our attention and time is scarce. Both creating and retrieving (reading/processing) complex maps is time-consuming and expensive.

REFLECTING ON YOUR EXISTING MODELS

All of us have already cultivated a number of existing mental tactics that we use on a daily basis. They might be simple or trivial. For example, you might put items that you frequently need, such as a pen, in the front of a drawer, and archive those that you don't need as frequently in the back (such as tax invoices). Other mental tactics might be more complex, and uncertain, such as models about human behaviour or self-identity. You might hold the belief that humans are generally self-interested and have selfish reasons for everything they do, even seemingly selfless deeds. If that's your map of the territory, you tend to think in terms of other's individual motives, their benefits, gains and losses.

It's important to be aware about your pre-existing maps and reflect on them frequently and consciously. Do they still hold up against the actual territory? By using them, are you able to make accurate forecasts about what's going to happen? In our seafarer's example, is the actual island that you discover recorded in the nautical maps? If it isn't, should you lose confidence in the map, discard it and look for a different one that fits reality better? Or should you adjust the map? The same holds true for mental tactics. Test them frequently, and be honest with yourself. When is it time to adjust the mental tactic? When should you discard it and look for a new, more effective one?

A SUMMARY OF THE MENTAL TACTICS IN THIS BOOK

We have tried to provide you with our 'best of' selection of mental tactics. We sincerely hope they provide valuable shortcuts for your work and life. If you've read *The Decision Maker's Playbook* chapter by chapter, you'll now have a strong toolkit that allows you to collect evidence, connect the dots, craft the solution and complete the mission more thoughtfully and effectively. We hope that you continue to adapt and refine these tactics to improve your decision making under changing circumstances.

Here's a short recap of the key insights in each chapter.

PART	CHAPTER	THE BOTTOM LINE
	Zero What's your problem?	Problems don't just exist, we actively choose and frame them. Good decision makers ask the 'Question Zero' first: What's my problem? Reflect on the framing of the problem: Who framed it? What are their underlying interests? And then think hard: Would this problem benefit from reframing? Should it be solved at all? Immediately? By me?

→

PART	CHAPTER	THE BOTTOM LINE
1	One Iluminate your blind spots: Admit what you don't know and correct your wrong beliefs	Humans don't have a built-in mechanism to detect false beliefs, or to be good at acknowledging what we don't know. Instead, we typically look for evidence to confirm our biases, and make up satisfying stories to fill in the gaps. To be a good problem solver, it is paramount to regularly review your belief system, calibrate confidence levels and actively practise humility.
	Two Bust your biases: See through the games your brain plays	Our minds use a lot of shortcuts to help us navigate the world. The problem is that most of these shortcuts are adapted for an environment that is long gone, and lead to biases in modern social settings. As far as gathering data and evidence is concerned, three types of biases are particularly relevant. First, simplification and stereotyping. Second, accepting stories that seem to make sense too quickly. Third, the inherent stickiness of the beliefs we hold. Actively de-biasing yourself takes time, but can be learned. It all starts with acknowledging the various distortions, being mindful and aware, as well as practising ways to deliberately shift down into System 2.
	Three Explore your data: Gather, scrutinise and visualise information to discover insights	The data you use to kick off your analysis will determine how useful your results are – and whether they are useful at all. Make sure that your data is good quality, and form hypotheses to make sense of your information. Always look for ways to go beyond the average and see the full picture of your data (by looking at descriptive statistics and forming views about the underlying distribution of your data). That's where the real insight is.
2	Four Drill down: Use tree diagrams to deconstruct any problem	Problems and data are often complex and messy. Tree diagrams provide a useful way to add structure to your thinking and give you a useful means of communication. Trees help you break down a trend or dynamic into their drivers, de-average aggregated numbers, find the root cause of a problem, or structure a presentation, project or vacation. Tree diagrams require you to think MECE (mutually exclusive, collectively exhaustive), and allow you to understand problems and data in a much deeper and clearer way.

→

PART	CHAPTER	THE BOTTOM LINE
	Five Move the needle: Anticipate regression to the mean	We are programmed to automatically look for patterns in data. But we often impose patterns on what is, in fact, random. Establishing rules that work reliably is difficult, particularly if you only have a few observations to build on, and if luck plays its part as well. To overcome regression to the mean, think about how much the success you are observing could be due to chance, hone counterfactual reasoning (what could have happened but didn't), and try to find more historical data points.
	Six See the big picture: Practise systems thinking	Systems are groups of interdependent actors or items forming an integrated whole. The environment, social groups and companies are all examples of systems. When mapping out systems, one typically starts by identifying causal chains such as A leads to B leads to C. Whenever C has an effect (directly or indirectly) on A, we call them feedback loops. Feedback loops result in emergent behaviour such as exponential growth (reinforcing feedback loops) or convergence (balancing feedback loops). Depending on your aim, you typically try to create, change or stop causal loops. The systems thinking mental tactic lets you analyse loops and find the most effective points of intervention.
3	Seven Think on the margin: Focus on the next unit	When we make decisions, we often take into account irrelevant factors such as costs incurred in the past. We often fall into the all or nothing trap in which we consider all the benefits and all the costs of a decision situation, which makes decision problems complex and unwieldy. Contrast that with marginal thinking. It requires you to only take into account variables pertinent to your current situation. In its core, marginal thinking is economic thinking, as it always assumes that decisions are made by weighing additional costs against additional benefits. Marginal thinking provides the foundation for rational decision making.
	Eight Score points: Articulate your criteria and make sound trade-offs	Many choices are not as straightforward as they seem at first. Equally, many decisions that appear complex or stressful can be radically simplified. Every option has a different set of advantages and disadvantages and often it's hard to pick the right one. A structured scoring model allows you to deliberately reflect on criteria, weights and scores, and provides you with a rigorous assessment approach. Using scoring models makes it easy to communicate and discuss choices and allows you to reach the most beneficial solution.

$\rightarrow$

PART	CHAPTER	THE BOTTOM LINE
	Nine Walk the talk: Run experiments to test your solutions in the real world	How do you know if your solution actually works? How can we make sure that our actions have the effect we intend? When it comes to understanding causal relationships, we typically revert to speculation, mimicking others or best practices. But the results often disappoint, because best practices may work in one situation but not in others. Experiments allow you to test your solutions and find out if they survive the crash with reality. Use randomised control trials (such as A/B tests) if you can randomise and have a large enough sample size for both control and treatment groups. Or apply n=1 experiments for situations with only one subject.
4	Ten Multiply your possibilities: Use real options to improve your odds of success	Having the option (but not the obligation) to act in the future is valuable, particularly in environments that change quickly and unpredictably, and that are hard to shape or influence. Options are everywhere you look. Understanding and valuing options is an important skill to hedge for future contingencies. Your goal should be to create and use them wisely to enable optimal decision making in the future. Remember, a truly valuable option hardly ever comes for free. Start thinking about your future choices as today's options, each with a value attached.
	Eleven Engineer incentives: Energise everyone to be their best	Incentives are tools to motivate individuals to perform actions. Misaligned incentives are one of the major causes of conflict and lost productivity in our world. However, careful up-front thought about the desired outcome, the relevant inputs and incentive system design can help anticipate and avoid common issues such as moral hazard, principal-agent and coordination problems. Pay attention to ineffective incentive systems and remember that intrinsic motivations may help you to change performance for the better, and for longer.
	Twelve Make it happen: Anticipate, execute and improve	Big things don't just happen. But with a little pre-planning, attention to action and post-action reflection, your most important projects can fall into place. The ability to plan and execute is a learned skill. It improves over time and with practice. Teams, individuals and groups increase their odds of success by putting in place techniques to plan effectively, execute well and reflect appropriately, such as the critical-path method, the pre-mortem and the decision audit.

TURNING IDEAS INTO ACTION

As we conclude this book, we're incredibly excited for you. We hope you had at least a few of the 'aha' moments we've enjoyed while collecting and refining these mental tactics over the years. Maybe you've learned about a mental tactic that you have witnessed in your work or life but didn't know how ubiquitous it was. Or, during reading, you realised how these models apply to problems you have experienced in the past.

The next step is to use these mental tactics in your future work and life. We write this as an invitation to start applying these concepts from today. To get you started, we want to offer the following suggestions:

- Over the next four weeks, use new problems as a trigger to slow down and consult this book. We typically rush into problem-solving mode, rather than stepping back and deliberately thinking about which mental tactics would best apply. Make the pledge to consciously use mental tactics, at least for a limited time – give them a chance.

- Take time to review and reflect on the mental tactic used in a particular situation. Did it serve as intended? Did it help to render your beliefs more accurately? Did it support you in spotting regressions to the mean? Did it help you focus on what makes the marginal difference?

- Find an accountability partner. Approach someone who's as invested in improving their problem-solving and decision-making skills as you are. Talk through problems together, and share new mental tactics with each other.

- Take our recommendations for other books and blogs to read on this subject. Please also see the suggested resources at the end of this book – they have all helped us tremendously.

This is only the beginning of the journey. Connecting and building mental tactics is a lifelong endeavour – worthwhile but demanding. We hope that you will start to build your own collection of ideas, concepts, frameworks and tools that help you make sense of this VUCA world. In doing that, aim for general fluency in selecting, reflecting and discarding mental tactics, not comprehensiveness. And keep on experimenting.

As we said at the beginning, this book can be read from start to finish, or as a reference guide, or a field manual, or an introductory text to concepts that we think are vitally important. It can also be *re-read* in any of these ways. We hope that you'll pick it up again and again – before a big meeting, at an inflection point in your life or when something happens that tickles your brain with a reminder of one or more of these mental tactics.

DON'T BE A STRANGER

The most meaningful part of our work is hearing from people who've put mental tactics into practice – how they use options to think about future decisions, their approach to calibrating their beliefs and their meta sense in thinking about problems. You are a part of that community now – the growing number of people who are fluent with these mental tactics and are passionate about applying them in work and life. Welcome to the club – we are delighted that you are here.

Please visit us online at **MentalTactics.com** and follow us on Twitter (**@MentalTactics**). We can't wait to hear where you take these ideas. Tell us:

- which of the concepts in this volume really resonated with you

- which ones you have put into practice and how you did it

- who you have shared these ideas with

- which experiments didn't work for you and any n=1 experiments that don't work out too (it is all data after all)

- which mental tactics not listed in this book you use on a frequent basis.

As you go out into the world, we make this invitation and request: think clearly, analyse rigorously, decide carefully, act boldly.

APPENDIX

Confidence calibration

—

In Chapter one, we talked about the importance of qualifying (and calibrating) the confidence levels of our beliefs.

To begin with, our beliefs should be *inherently* uncertain. But this is not how we typically form opinions. Instead, when we are convinced of something, we instinctively attach a 100% confidence level to it. Expressing beliefs in probabilities needs to be practised. It is not what we do automatically.

Once it has become a habit to express your beliefs in probabilities, you should calibrate your belief system so that your probabilities are reliable and useful. But how do you go about calibrating your beliefs in a systematic fashion? Essentially, you will need to give answers to a number of questions and provide your subjective confidence level for each.

A sample question could be: "How many countries are members of the United Nations? Provide the range at a confidence level of 90%." An answer to that question consists of an upper and lower boundary of that number. And 90% confidence means that if you were to repeat a question similar to this one, the *true* number would only be outside of the range that you specified once every 10 times. The Center for Applied Rationality (CFAR) has come up with an online Credence Calibration Game that comprises many questions like the ones above and allows you to measure your confidence.[83]

Another way is to start a long list of your own predictions. How sure are you that something will happen within a given time period, say one year? Write down what you expect will have happened at the end of the year. Do this exercise in the weeks around New Year's Eve. Of course, you could also choose a smaller unit of time, such as a project, holiday or some other time interval. As you note down your projections, make sure they are binary – they can be answered with true or false, or simply yes or no. In addition, note down how confident you are.

A list could look like this.

BELIEF	HOW CONFIDENT?
No new competitor will enter our market	80%
President X will not be impeached	90%
The value of our house will rise by more than 5%	60%

Do this for a large number of beliefs, say 50 to 100, and make sure you have plenty of predictions for each confidence *level* (i.e. at least 5 for the confidence level 80%).

At the end of the year, you can revisit your beliefs and mark if they were true or not. Simply add a column to your table to indicate whether or not the prediction was correct or incorrect.

BELIEF	HOW CONFIDENT?	DID IT COME TRUE?
No new competitor will enter our market	80%	*Yes*, the competitive set is unchanged
President X will not be impeached	90%	*Yes*, President X is still in office
The value of our house will rise by more than 5%	60%	*No*, the price of our house went up only 3%

After noting down how the individual predictions turned out, plotting confidence levels on a graph will allow you to identify where you've been over or underconfident.

Start with an empty graph similar to the one below.

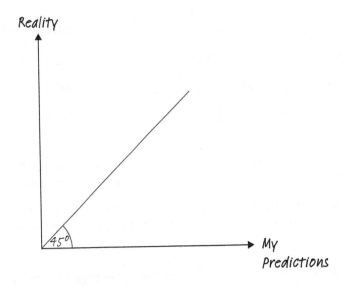

This chart will allow you to represent your predictions in a visual way and compare them against reality.

Aggregate all your predictions into 'buckets' of confidence. Start with the 50% bucket (predictions you were as confident about as a coin toss). How many of those predictions have come true? Enter that percentage as a percentage of all predictions on the y-axis.

Then continue with the next bucket of predictions, the ones where you indicated a confidence level of 60%. Proceed in a similar fashion. Take a look at all your predictions or beliefs that you are 60% confident about and calculate the percentage of those predictions [*actually*] *matching reality.* Find that point on the plot and mark it.

Continue with the rest of the confidence levels: 70%, 80%, 90% and 100% (completely sure that something will happen or something is true).

Connect the dots on your graph and compare them with the optimal 45-degree line. Whenever a dot is *below* the 45-degree line, you are *overconfident* at that confidence level. A dot below the 45-degree line means you were more confident than warranted. Whenever it is *above* the line, you are *underconfident.*

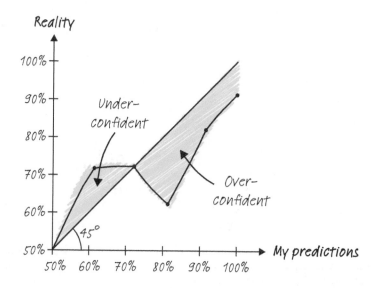

Repeat this exercise frequently to keep your beliefs about the world well-calibrated and challenge overconfidence.

You can use this method not only to hold yourself accountable, but also to do the same with experts and pundits. Compare their prediction with what turned out to be true.[84]

By the way, here is Simon's graph of predictions made for the year 2017.

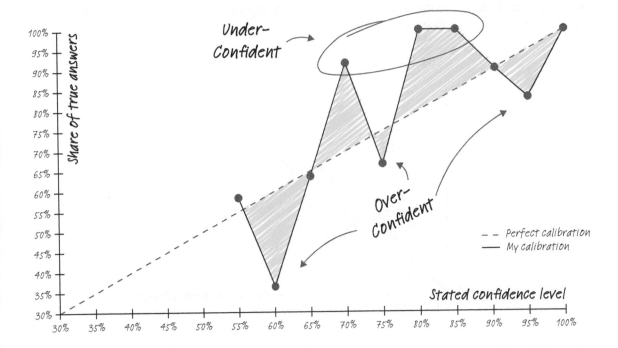

FURTHER RESOURCES

—

Books

- Albert-Laszlo Barabasi and Jennifer Frangos: *Linked: The New Science of Networks* (2002)
- Daniel Kahneman: *Thinking, Fast and Slow* (2011)
- Darrell Huff and Irving Geis: *How to Lie with Statistics* (1993)
- Donella H. Meadows and Diana Wright: *Thinking in Systems: A Primer* (2009)
- Douglas W.Hubbard: *How to Measure Anything* (2010)
- Duncan J. Watts: *Everything is Obvious* (2011)
- Eliezer Yudkowsky: *Rationality – From AI to Zombies* (2015)
- Jordan Ellenberg: *How Not to Be Wrong* (2015)
- Kevin Simler and Robin Hanson: *The Elephant in the Brain* (2017)
- Marvin Minsky: *The Society of Mind* (1986)
- Michael J. Mauboussin: *The Success Equation* (2012)
- Nassim Taleb: *Fooled by Randomness* (2005)
- Philip Tetlock and Dan Gardner: *Superforecasting* (2015)
- Richard Feynman: *Surely You're Joking, Mr Feynman! Adventures of a Curious Character* (1985)
- Richard Thaler and Cass Sunstein: *Nudge* (2008)
- Steven Pinker: *How the Mind Works* (1999)

Websites and podcasts

- lesswrong.com
- 80000hours.org
- rationality.org
- overcomingbias.com
- marginalthinking.com
- PaulGraham.com
- samharris.org/podcast
- rationallyspeakingpodcast.org
- ted.com/read/ted-podcasts/worklife

NOTES
—

Front Matter

1 Our choice of the term 'mental tactics' is influenced by the work of Alfred Korzybski, who has done trailblazing work in the field of general semantics. He is well-known for his assertion "the map is not the territory" (Korzybski, A. (1958) Science and Sanity: An Introduction to Non-Aristotelian Systems and General Semantics, p. 58. Institute of GS.)

2 Charlie Chaplin: Modern Times (1936), distributed by: United Artists (UA) https://en .wikipedia.org/wiki/Modern_Times_(film)]

3 Stiehm, Judith H. (2010) *US Army War College: Military Education in a Democracy*, Temple University Press.

Chapter Zero

4 Meng Zhu, Yang Yang, Hsee, Christopher K. (2018) 'The Mere Urgency Effect', *Journal of Consumer Research*. [Online] Volume 45 (3, October). p. 673–90. Available from: https:// doi.org/10.1093/jcr/ucy008 [Accessed: 24 June 2019].

5 Dwight Eisenhower presented a version of the adage in a 1954 speech at Northwestern University in Evanston, Illinois to the Second Assembly of the World Council of Churches, in which he credited an unnamed former college president for it.

6 This idea is known as 'earning to give' and is part of a wider philanthropic movement called 'effective altruism'.

7 For a a good discussion on how to evaluate the true impact of career choices, the website https://80000hours.org is the go-to-place.

Chapter One

8 The idea was first developed by Peter Wason, an experimental psychologist, in 1960: Wason, P.C. (1960) 'On the failure to eliminate hypotheses in a conceptual task', *Quarterly Journal of Experimental Psychology*, 12(3), pp. 129–40.

9 Kahneman, D., Lovallo, D. and Sibony, O. (2011) 'Before you make that big decision', *Harvard Business Review,* 89(6), pp.50–60.

10 Watt, C.S. (2017) '"There's no future for taxis": New York yellow cab drivers drowning in debt'. *The Guardian*. [Online] 20 October. Available from: www.theguardian.com/us-news/2017/oct/20/new-york-yellow-cab-taxi-medallion-value-cost. [Accessed 24 June 2019].

11 Byrne, J.A. (2018) '139 taxi medallions will be offered at bankruptcy auction'. *New York Post*. [Online] Available from: https://nypost.com/2018/06/09/139-taxi-medallions-will-be-offered-at-bankruptcy-auction. [Accessed: 18 May 2019].

12 Centers for Disease Control and Prevention. (2017) 'Morbidity and Mortality Weekly Report: Measles Outbreak — Minnesota April–May 2017'. [Online] Available from: www .cdc.gov/mmwr/volumes/66/wr/mm6627a1. [Accessed: 24 October 2018].

13 For further reading, we recommend Bazerman, M. (2014) *The Power of Noticing: What the Best Leaders See*. Simon & Schuster.

14 The display of great confidence matches the profile of prototypical leaders, which leads group members to choose narcissists in group settings. But even though they are perceived as more effective, they actually diminish group performance. See Nevicka, B, Ten Velden, F.S., De Hoogh, AH and Van Vianen, AE (2011) 'Reality at odds with perceptions: Narcissistic leaders and group performance', *Psychological Science*, 22(10), pp.1259–64.

15 Kruger, J. and Dunning, D. (1999) 'Unskilled and Unaware of it: How Difficulties in Recognizing One's Own Incompetence Lead to Inflated Self-Assessments', *Journal of Personality and Social Psychology*, 77(6), p.1121.

16 This expression has been popularised by then US Secretary of Defense Donald Rumsfeld in his news briefing about the thin evidence base linking Iraq with weapons of mass destruction. It can be traced back to the work of the two psychologists Joseph Luft and Harrington Ingham.

17 Hall, L. et al. (2010) 'Magic at the marketplace: Choice blindness for the taste of jam and the smell of tea', *Cognition*, 117(1), pp.54–61.

18 Dennett, D.C. (2013) *Intuition pumps and other tools for thinking*. W.W. Norton & Company.

19 Richard Feynman, American theoretical physicist (1918–88).

20 Tabarrock, A. (2012) 'A bet is a tax on bullshit'. Marginal Revolution. [Online] 2 November. Available from: https://marginalrevolution.com/marginalrevolution/2012/11/a-bet-is-a-tax-on-bullshit.html. [Accessed: 10 November 2018].

21 Sagan, C. (1979) *Broca's Brain, Reflections on the Romance of Science*. New York: Random House.

22 O'Connor, A. (2017) 'Sugar Industry Long Downplayed Potential Harms'. *The New York Times*. [Online] 21 November. Available from: www.nytimes.com/2017/11/21/well/eat/sugar-industry-long-downplayed-potential-harms-of-sugar.html. [Accessed: 3 April 2018].

23 Kicinski, M. (2013) 'Publication bias in recent meta-analyses', *PloS one, 8*(11), p.e81823.

24 Zenko, M. (2015) 'Inside the CIA Red Cell: How an experimental unit transformed the intelligence community'. *Foreign Policy*. [Online] 30 October. Available from: http://foreignpolicy.com/2015/10/30/inside-the-cia-red-cell-micah-zenko-red-team-intelligence/. [Accessed: 18 November 2018].

Chapter Two

25 The dual processing theory had its beginning in the work of William James, and branched out from there. James, W. (1890) *The Principles of Psychology*. New York: Henry Holt & Co. Vol. 1, p.673.

26 For much more on System 1 and System 2 processing, we recommend Nobel laureate Daniel Kahneman's superb book, *Thinking, Fast and Slow*: Kahneman, D and Egan, P (2011) New York: Farrar, Straus and Giroux.

27 For a regularly updated and fairly comprehensive list, we suggest Wikipedia's *List of Cognitive Biases*. Available at: https://en.wikipedia.org/wiki/List_of_cognitive_biases. For a more visual view refer to Buster Benson's 'Cognitive Biases Cheat Sheet'. Available at: https://betterhumans.coach.me/cognitive-bias-cheat-sheet-55a472476b18.

28 Tversky, A., and Kahneman, D. (1983) 'Extensional Versus Intuitive Reasoning: The Conjunction Fallacy in Probability Judgment', *Psychology Review 90*, 4. doi: 10.1037/0033-295X.90.4.293.

29 Carlon Rush, B. (2014) 'Science of storytelling: why and how to use it in your marketing'. *The Guardian*. [Online] 28 August. Available from: www.theguardian.com/media-network/media-network-blog/2014/aug/28/science-storytelling-digital-marketing. [Accessed: 2 December 2018].

30 Baron, J. and Hershey, J.C. (1988) 'Outcome Bias in Decision Evaluation'. *Journal of Personality and Social Psychology* Vol. 54, No. 4, pp.569–79. Available at: http://commonweb.unifr.ch/artsdean/pub/gestens/f/as/files/4660/21931_171009.pdf. [Accessed: 25 June 2019].

31 Project Implicit. [Online] Available from: https://implicit.harvard.edu/implicit/. [Accessed: 1 December 2018].

32 For those interested to dive much deeper into the science behind the Implicit Association Test, we recommend *Banaji, M.R. and Greenwald, A.G.* Delacorte Press (2013).

33 Morourke (2018) 'Worker Centers & OUR Walmart: Case studies on the changing face of labor in the United States'. The Case Studies Blog, Harvard Law School. [Online] 19 June. Available from: https://blogs.harvard.edu/hlscasestudies/2014/12/02/hbs-shares-how-to-make-class-discussions-fair/. [Accessed: 25 June 2019].

Chapter Three

34 Rich, N. (2013), 'Silicon Valley's Start-Up Machine'. *The New York Times Magazine.* [Online] 2 May. Available from: https://www.nytimes.com/2013/05/05/magazine/y-combinator-silicon-valleys-start-up-machine.html. [Accessed: 11 November 2018].

35 Rich, N. (2013) 'Silicon Valley's Start-Up Machine'. *The New York Times Magazine.* [Online] 2 May. Available from: www.nytimes.com/2013/05/05/magazine/y-combinator-silicon-valleys-start-up-machine.html. [Accessed: 18 November 2018].

36 Azoulay, P., Jones, B., Daniel Kim, J. and Miranda, J. (2018) 'Research: The Average Age of a Successful Startup Founder Is 45'. *Harvard Business Review.* [Online] 11 July. Available from: https://hbr.org/2018/07/research-the-average-age-of-a-successful-startup-founder-is-45. [Accessed: 18 November 2018].

37 The best guide we know to structured thinking, not only quantitative problem solving, but better organised thinking in general is Barbara Minto's *The Pyramid Principle.* Originally published in 1978, it is what Australians would call "an oldie but a goodie". Minto, B. (2009) *The Pyramid Principle: Logic in Writing and Thinking.* Pearson Education.

38 The problem of missing data is of deep interest to research scientists, data analysts and systems engineers and should be of importance to all of us. For a deep dive on missing data, see Raghunathan, T. (2015) *Missing Data Analysis in Practice.* Chapman and Hall/CRC.

39 For much more on distributions, we recommend Tegmark, M. (2014) *Our Mathematical Universe: My Quest for the Ultimate Nature of Reality.* Vintage.

40 Crockett, Z. (2015) 'The most prolific editor on Wikipedia'. Priceonomics. [Online] 14 October. Available from: https://priceonomics.com/the-most-prolific-editor-on-wikipedia/. [Accessed: 20 February 2019].

Chapter Five

41 Marcus Aurelius, Meditations, IV, 3

42 The way we describe the trade-offs between skill and luck in this chapter are inspired by Michael Mauboussin's book *The Success Equation*, a much more comprehensive treatise on this subject: Mauboussin, M.J. (2012) *The Success Equation: Untangling Skill and Luck in Business, Sports, and Investing*. Harvard Business Press.

43 Each circle in the chart depicts the average height of two parents and their child. Results are grouped in increments of one inch, which leads to overlaps.

44 Galton, F. (1886) 'Regression towards mediocrity in hereditary stature', *The Journal of the Anthropological Institute of Great Britain and Ireland*, 15, pp.246–63.

45 Collins, J.C. (2001) *Good to Great: Why Some Companies Make the Leap … and Others Don't*. New York, NY: HarperBusiness.

46 Henderson, A.D., Raynor, M.E. and Ahmed, M. (2012) 'How long must a firm be great to rule out chance? Benchmarking sustained superior performance without being fooled by randomness', *Strategic Management Journal*, 33(4), pp.387–406.

47 Mauboussin, Michael J. (2012) 'The Success Equation: Untangling Skill and Luck in Business, Sports, and Investing', *Harvard Business Review Press*.

Chapter Six

48 Meadows, D.H. (2008) *Thinking in Systems: A Primer*. Chelsea Green Publishing, p. 2.

49 The R in the centre of the graphic indicates the type of the feedback loop (reinforcing) and its direction (clockwise).

50 A modified example from Kim, D.H. (1994) *Systems Archetypes II: Using Systems Archetypes to Take Effective Action* (Vol. 2). Pegasus Communications.

51 This example is inspired by the works of J.D. Moizer (1999) in *System Dynamics Modelling of Occupational Safety: A Case Study Approach*.

52 Merriam-Webster. Definition of system. Available from: www.merriam-webster.com/dictionary/system [Accessed: 15 April 2018].

Chapter Seven

53 Stevenson, B. and Wolfers, J. (2008) *Economic Growth and Subjective Well-being: Reassessing the Easterlin Paradox*. NBER Working Paper No. 14282.

Chapter Eight

54 For much more on alternatives, we recommend Johnson, S. (2018) *Farsighted: How We Make the Decisions that Matter the Most.* Penguin.

55 For more on this topic, we recommend Paul Nutt's excellent book: Nutt, P. (2002) *Why Decisions Fail: Avoiding the Blunders and Traps that Lead to Debacles.* Berrett-Koehler Publishers.

56 For more details backing up this claim, see Hubbard, D.W. (2010) *How to Measure Anything: Finding the Value of Intangibles in Business.* John Wiley & Sons.

57 Not true of course, Simon is very safety-conscious!

58 This table and all related calculations can be downloaded from DecisionMakersPlaybook. com

Chapter Nine

59 Thomke, S. and Manzi, J. (2014) 'The discipline of business experimentation'. *Harvard Business Review.* 92(12), p.17.

60 Branwen, G. (2008) 'Melatonin improves sleep, & sleep is valuable'. Melatonin. [Online] 19 December. Available from: https://www.gwern.net/Melatonin. [Accessed: 7 November 2018].

61 Experiments with a sample size of 1.

62 Augemberg, K. (2012) 'Quantified Self How-To: Designing Self-Experiments'. *h+ Magazine.* [Online] 14 November. Available from: http://hplusmagazine.com/2012/11/14/quantified-self-how-to-designing-self-experiments/. [Accessed: 25 June 2019]

Chapter Ten

63 Damodaran, A. (2007) *Strategic Risk Taking: A Framework for Risk Management.* Pearson Prentice Hall, p.262.

64 Let's assume that only outside influences (such as family events or job offers in other cities) will determine the duration of her stay. We have further simplified this decision tree by only giving Annie 2 options: staying for the whole time or leaving after 12 months.

65 The option to abandon is closely related to the option to contract. Similar to the option to switch, the option to contract is basically the right to walk away from a project if certain conditions are unfavourable (unlike the option to switch, the option to contract does not include a right to resume operations).

Chapter Eleven

66 Most political scientists and economists would argue that the principal-agent problem is a variant of moral hazard. We don't disagree. In practice, though, principal-agent problems are both so frequent and potentially detrimental that we think they deserve their own category.

67 The 2007 subprime mortgage crisis is one of the best possible educations on misaligned incentives in recent memory. For further reading, see Bethany McLean and Joe Nocera's *All The Devils Are Here* (2010), Portfolio Press and Michael Lewis' *The Big Short* (2010), W.W. Norton & Company.

68 Indeed, this specific dilemma is responsible for the entire professional category of the independent financial advisor, who receives no compensation or rewards from anyone but the immediate client, in an effort to cancel out the principal-agent dilemma.

69 For a beautiful and extremely positive take on how to use loss aversion to lift performance, see Rosamund Stone Zander and Benjamin Zander's book: Zander, R.S. and Zander B. (2002) *The Art of Possibility Transforming Professional and Personal Life.* Penguin Books.

70 Strathern, M. (1997) 'Improving ratings: audit in the British University system'. *European Review* 5. pp.305–21.

71 Bareket-Bojmel, L., Hochman, G. and Ariely, D. (2017) 'It's (not) all about the Jacksons: testing different types of short-term bonuses in the field'. Journal of Management. 43(2), pp.534–54.

72 For more wisdom like it, we recommend Dan Ariely's lovely little book: Ariely, D. (2016) *Payoff: The Hidden Logic That Shapes Our Motivations.* TED Books.

73 See Chip Health's article: Health, C. (1999) 'On the Social Psychology of Agency Relationships: Lay Theories of Motivation Overemphasize Extrinsic Incentives'. *Organizational Behavior and Human Decision Processes.* Vol. 78, No. 1, pp. 25–62.

74 Deci, E.L., Koestner, R. and Ryan, R.M. (1999) 'A meta-analytic review of experiments examining the effects of extrinsic rewards on intrinsic motivation'. *Psychological Bulletin.* 125(6), p.627.

Chapter Twelve

75 Kahneman, D. and Tversky, A. (1979) 'Intuitive Prediction: Biases and Corrective Procedures'. TIMS Studies in Management Science. 12: 313–27.

76 Blenko, M., Mankins, M. and Rogers, P. (2010) 'The Decision-Driven Organization'. *Harvard Business Review*. [Online] June. Available from: https://hbr.org/2010/06/the-decision-driven-organisation.

77 Prasad, V. (2010) 'Reclaiming the morbidity and mortality conference: between Codman and Kundera'. *Medical Humanities*. 36(2), pp.108–11.

78 Di Stefano, G., Gino, F., Pisano, G.P. and Staats, B.R. (2016) *Making Experience Count: The Role of Reflection in Individual Learning*. Harvard Business School.

Chapter Thirteen

79 Y Combinator. Available from: https://old.ycombinator.com/munger.html. [Accessed: 21 November 2018].

80 For much more on how dating and human relationships have transformed in the last century, we recommend Ansari, A. and Klinenberg, E. (2015) *Modern Romance*. Penguin.

81 A phrase frequently used by the excellent historian Y.N. Harari: Hariri, Y.N. (2018) *21 Lessons for the 21st Century*. Random House.

82 As above: we credit Alfred Korzybski for this phrase. Korzybski, A. (1958) *'Science and Sanity: An Introduction to Non-Aristotelian Systems and General Semantics'*. Institute of GS. p.58.

Appendix

83 Critch, A. (2012) 'The Credence Calibration Game, by CFAR – an overview'. Available from: http://acritch.com/credence-game/. [Accessed: 9 December 2018].

84 On predictions specifically, we highly recommend Philip Tetlock's and Dan Gardner's book Tetlock, P. and Gardner, D. (2016) *Superforecasting: The Art and Science of Prediction*. Random House Books. It synthesises findings from The Good Judgment Project, which showed that specifically selected amateur forecasters were often more accurately tuned than pundits or subject-matter experts. Tetlock, P.E. and Gardner, D. (2016) *Superforecasting: The Art and Science of Prediction*. Random House.

INDEX

—